Affiliate Marketing

Learn

How To Make

$10,000+ Each Month

On Autopilot!

By

Michael Ezeanaka

www.MichaelEzeanaka.com

Copyright ©2019

Disclaimer

This publication is designed to provide competent and reliable information regarding the subject matter covered. However, it is sold with the understanding that the author is not engaged in rendering investment or other professional advice. Laws and practices often vary from state to state and country to country and if investment or other expert assistance is required, the services of a professional should be sought. The author specifically disclaims any liability that is incurred from the use or application of the contents of this book.

Books In The Business and Money Series	
Series #	**Book Title**
1	Affiliate Marketing
2	Passive Income Ideas
3	Affiliate Marketing + Passive Income Ideas (2-in-1 Bundle)
4	Facebook Advertising
5	Dropshipping
6	Dropshipping + Facebook Advertising (2-in-1 Bundle)
7	Real Estate Investing For Beginners
8	Credit Cards and Credit Repair Secrets
9	Real Estate Investing And Credit Repair Strategies (2-in-1 Bundle)
10	Passive Income With Affiliate Marketing (2nd Edition)
11	Passive Income With Dividend Investing
12	Stock Market Investing For Beginners
13	The Simple Stock Market Investing Blueprint (2-in-1 Bundle)
14	Real Estate And Stock Market Investing Mastery (3-in-1 Bundle)

The kindle edition will be available to you for FREE when you purchase the paperback version from Amazon.com (The US Store)

Download The Audio Versions Along With The Complementary PDF Document For FREE from www.MichaelEzeanaka.com > My Audiobooks

Table of Contents

Traffic Optimization Secrets

If you want a handy booklet that reveals traffic optimization secrets you can use to drive massive amounts of traffic to your affiliate offer then you are in luck! A PDF version of the below book is located at a certain place and can be downloaded for FREE. However, a password is required to unlock the download. Follow the steps below to retrieve the password!

Steps to take

1. The password consists of 7 characters (all lower case)
2. Here is the incomplete password: f-y-z-x
3. The **second**, **fourth** and **sixth** character of the password is missing and is located in random pages of this book.
4. **Read this book** carefully to locate and retrieve them (they're so obvious you can't miss them).
5. Once you have the complete password then go to www.MichaelEzeanaka.com
6. Navigate to Free Stuff > Ebooks/Audiobooks > Traffic Optimization Secrets
7. Enter the password, download the booklet and enjoy!

Introduction

Are you looking for an online business that you can start today? If so, affiliate marketing is for you. This method of earning money through the Internet has been around for more than two decades and people are still using the same model today as 20 years ago.

This book will teach you everything you need to know about affiliate marketing. It discusses how it all started and evolved to the multi-billion dollar industry that it is today.

In this book, we will discuss how you can get your slice of the affiliate marketing pie. You will learn how you can start with this business and build your affiliate marketing assets from scratch. You will also learn how to develop content and drive massive amounts of traffic to them through organic (free) and paid methods.

Lastly, we talk about the different strategies on how you can become successful as an Internet marketer and how you can **earn a lot of money** with Affiliate Marketing. With the help of this book, you will be on your way to earn a *six-figure* monthly income.

Start building your affiliate marketing empire today!

Inspiration #1

"There are no secrets to success. It is the result of preparation, hard work, and learning from failure."

Colin Powell

Chapter 1

What Is Affiliate Marketing?

Affiliate marketing refers to programs that aim to sell more products for a company through partnerships with third party online sales people called affiliates or publishers. Unlike traditional Contextual Advertising, affiliate marketing programs allow content publishers to connect directly with advertisers.

A successful affiliate marketing campaign can lead to a higher income to publishers compared to publishing contextual ads from services like Google AdSense. From an advertiser's standpoint, affiliate marketing is an efficient way of promoting one's products because the reward system is based on the publisher's productivity. The advertiser only needs to pay if the publisher successfully facilitates a sale.

History of Affiliate marketing

The affiliate marketing business model is not new. It has been around shortly after the first few businesses started offering products and services in the web. The affiliate marketing commission system was likely inspired by the commission payment system of offline sales people. In the sales world outside the internet, sales people have been paid via commission or a percentage of the payment amount for the longest time. In particular, it is a common sales model in the cosmetic, homeware, car and pharmaceutical industries.

The first recorded transition of this business model to the online world happened in 1994. It was a flower selling business called PC Flowers and Gifts. Its founder, William J. Tobin, designed and patented the use of revenue sharing and tracking of visitor's activities. The first affiliate network was the Prodigy Network, an IBM owned subscription service that offered online services like access to news, games, polls and many more. Subscribers of the network were given the opportunity to earn commission for facilitating a PC Flowers and Gifts sale to other members of the network.

In 1996, Amazon launched what we now call Amazon associates. At the time, Amazon focused on selling tangible books. A website owner can post a banner ad or a link that leads directly to the product page of a specific book. Commission is paid if a visitor who used the link purchases the book.

In the years that followed, many other affiliate marketing schemes were launched but Amazon Associates became the most popular among them. Since then, the popularity of affiliate marketing as a website monetization method has increased. In 2006 for instance, sales generated by affiliate marketing in the UK, amounted to $2.92 billion.

The popularity of affiliate marketing increased even more when more and more people took part in online content creation. In the early 2000s, Web 2.0 types of content became increasingly popular online. People turned to blogs and forums for answers when they face problems. Some of these blogs and forums monetized their online properties using affiliate marketing programs. By positioning affiliate products as a solution to people's problems, they were able to earn from the content they post on their websites.

Around 2011, Google cleaned up its search engine results pages with what is commonly called the Panda update. This update in the search algorithm penalized websites with poor content. This was largely due to the fact that many website owners gamed the process of ranking in Google's search result pages. This process is called Search Engine Optimization or SEO.

By doing practices frowned upon by Google, webmasters with websites that hardly have any useful content in them managed to reach the top spot of search result pages. Practices like stuffing a webpage with keywords or creating thousands of fake links that point to a websites allowed these webmasters to raise their spam webpages in the rankings. Most of these spam webpages were monetized by affiliate links and banners. With Google cracking down on webpages like these, the black hat days of most affiliate marketers came to an end.

After the Google Panda updates, websites that provided useful and engaging content rose to fill the top positions of the search result pages. Because of this, websites with excellent content managed to get the affiliate marketing sales.

In the following years, affiliate marketers saw the emergence of social media websites. Together with this, smartphones and other mobile devices replaced personal computers as the primary tools used for accessing the internet. With these changes in the internet marketing world, affiliate marketing strategies also evolved. The internet became a truly multimedia experience. Text content no longer ruled the internet. Instead, videos and images dominated the screens of internet users.

This gave way to a new breed of affiliate marketers. Some of them do not even own a website. They only use their Facebook pages, YouTube Channels and Instagram accounts to generate affiliate sales. These days, people no longer spend countless hours surfing the web. Instead, they stick to one or two apps, fully engaged in the content in these apps. This is the current state of affiliate marketing. The old ways of succeeding in this business still has some value. You could still earn by posting useful content in your website. However, if you want your affiliate marketing game to improve, you need to master the social media-marketing world as well.

The Affiliate marketing business model

As we discussed above, affiliate marketing is a revenue sharing business model designed to increase the sales of a particular product or service. Before we talk about how you can take part in this business model, let us first discuss the different players in this type of business:

The Advertiser

To understand affiliate marketing, one needs to understand the three parties involved in this type of marketing program. The first one, is the advertiser or the business that wants to promote its products or services. They set up their own affiliate marketing program or they sign up with an affiliate network to manage the marketing program for them. The advertiser's goal is simply to sell more products and to reach new markets through the internet. Most of the time, they set up this kind of program because they want to reach online markets that they normally cannot reach by traditional online advertising.

Affiliate marketing also has other benefits for the advertiser's online presence. By setting up this program, more content creators will be talking about their products. Some of these content creators have thousands of fans. Each one of these followers will be exposed to their products. Even if these followers do not purchase a product now, they will still become familiar with the promoted product. They may choose to look for the product in the future, without passing through the affiliate marketing channel.

The advertisers should provide the tools needed by the publishers. For instance, they could provide marketing materials that the affiliate publishers will use to promote their products. They should also provide the platform to make it easier for the publisher to participate in the program. Most affiliate programs come with an account to the affiliate marketing website. This website serves as source of all the tools provided by the advertiser. It also comes with a dashboard where the publisher can tract their performance.

The consumers

The next party in the affiliate marketing business model is the consumers. The consumers refer to the people who buy the products of the advertiser. The advertisers want the right types of consumers to see their marketing materials. If they like the advertiser's product or service, they can click on the link provided with the marketing material and start the purchasing process.

The internet is filled with people who can become consumers. However, the best types of consumers are those that are willing and able to buy the advertiser's products. A willing consumer is interested in the product or service. He or she has a personal reason for wanting or needing the product. A consumer is able to buy the product if he or she can complete the purchasing process. First, the consumer needs to have the technical knowhow on completing an online purchase. He or she should also have enough funds to pay for the product or service offered.

The Publisher

The last party is the publishers. Publishers are the people who post the marketing materials of the advertisers so that the consumers can view them. Affiliate programs usually require their publishers to have an online asset that they can use to attract the attention of consumers. Most affiliate programs require that you have a website where you will promote their products or services. While a website is usually required when signing up, the publisher is not limited to promoting the advertiser's marketing materials in there. Depending on the affiliate program guidelines, the publisher can use contextual advertising, social media marketing, and other means to bring attention to the affiliate offer.

If you want to earn money in affiliate marketing, the best way is to become a publisher. It will be your role to generate leads towards the websites of your affiliate advertisers. This means that you need to attract people who are likely to buy the products of the advertisers and encourage them to go to the advertiser website and make a purchase.

This part however, is easier said than done. Though billions of people use the internet every day, you will not be able to reach the majority of them. A big chunk of the online population does not speak English. Among the English speakers, only a small percentage is interested in the topics you are discussing in your blog, your videos or your podcasts. Even among people who are interested in the topic you are discussing, only a small percentage have intentions of buying online. The majority of people still prefer to buy things through brick-and-mortar stores if they are available. Many of those who habitually buy things online have their preferred online stores. Many of them just buy from the popular sources like Amazon.

The most successful publishers earn through affiliate marketing consistently by establishing themselves as authorities in their chosen fields. You may also follow this path. Most of these people are already experts in their fields and they only use online marketing as a source of extra income. If you want to create content related to your job for example, you can brand yourself as an expert. A trainer in a gym for example, can create a website where he puts contents that gym goers can do when they cannot go to his classes. In the process, he can promote fitness related products that the visitors of his website can make use of. Because the gym trainer is an expert in his field, the visitors in his website are likely to follow his advice.

You can also take the same approach by starting an affiliate business based on what you do for a living or on a hobby you like to do. By doing so, you can establish yourself as an expert in that field. It will also be easier for you to find your first website followers. You can encourage the people you meet in your job to visit your website. In there, you can provide free advice to keep the visitors coming back to your website. In the process, you can monetize the website by suggesting products and services that you use yourself. You could then use affiliate links to direct your visitors to these products and services.

A carpenter for example, could provide free carpentry lessons in his website and his social media accounts. Together with his content, he could provide Amazon Associate links to the product pages of the tools and other products that he uses in his carpentry lessons.

To establish yourself as an expert, you will need to provide evidence to the visitors of your website. For instance, you can create an about page where you put your credentials and your achievements in the field. You could also provide photos where in you are working to show people that you are who you say you are.

While it is easier to convince people to buy the affiliate products if you are an expert, there are other approaches to become a trusted source in the affiliate marketing business. For instance, you can also become a successful publisher even if you are just a beginner at your chosen topic. Instead of providing advice based on your personal experience, you can also give them as you learn a new topic. A beginner carpenter for example could show people his journey in learning to become an expert. In the process, he could share the lessons he learned together with the tools he uses to learn.

Many people who go to the internet are beginners who want to learn something. It is rare to see a free website that will teach you everything you need to know to learn a skill. Most websites that teach specific skills tend to be paid and often demand a high price. You can give the audience a free version of these websites. Instead of charging the people for the information, you can earn through the affiliate marketing income instead.

Congratulations!

The second character of the password required to unlock the Traffic Optimization Secrets booklet is letter a.

Chapter 1 Quiz
Please refer to Appendix A for the answers to this quiz

1. What do you call productivity-based programs that partner with online sellers to encourage the sale of products and services?

    A) Contextual marketing
    B) Affiliate Marketing
    C) Cost Per Click Marketing
    D) Search Marketing

2. What do you call the third-party sellers that promote affiliate products to consumers?

    A) Advertisers
    B) Online Sellers
    C) Affiliates
    D) Programmers

3. Where did the commissions payment system used in affiliate marketing originate?

    A) Real-world sales industry
    B) Online contextual advertising industry
    C) Email marketing
    D) The bakeshop business

4. When was the first affiliate marketing program started?

    A) 1994
    B) 1996
    C) 1991
    D) 1998

5. When was Amazon Associates launched?

    A) 1994
    B) 1996
    C) 1991
    D) 1998

6. What are businesses that set up affiliate programs called?

    A) Affiliates
    B) Advertisers

C) Business Partners

D) Consumers

7. What do you call the percentage of the purchase price paid to the affiliate?

   A) Success Rate

   B) Commission Rate

   C) Conversion Rate

   D) Payment Method

8. Who are the general target audience of affiliate programs?

   A) Children

   B) Business owners

   C) Advertisers

   D) Consumer

9. What are the two requirements of an ideal product consumer?

   A) Willingness and capacity to buy

   B) Social media and search engine usage

   C) Facebook account and credit card

   D) Computer and twitter account

10. How are affiliate marketers paid?

   A) Commission System

   B) An agreed upon fixed amount

   C) Based on the cost per click rate

   D) Based on the number of impressions

Inspiration #2

"If you really want to do something, you'll find a way. If you don't, you'll find an excuse."

Jim Rohn

Chapter 2:

Low Ticket vs. High Ticket Affiliate Marketing

If you want to become an affiliate marketer, there are many products and services you can choose from. Veteran affiliate marketers classify these products based on their prices. The price of the promoted product is important to the affiliate marketer because the commissions they earn are usually a percentage of the product's selling price. With this in mind, affiliate marketers classify low cost products as low-ticket affiliate products and those that are more expensive to be high-ticket affiliate products.

As you start in the affiliate marketing business, you need to decide whether you want to promote cheap or expensive items. Most affiliate marketers choose to promote low-ticket affiliate products because they think that it is easier to convince people to buy cheap items. However, this also means that you need to sell *A LOT* more items to reach your income goals.

Let's say you have a website that promotes small bedroom items. The average price of the products you promote is $5 and you earn a 10% commission for each sale you promote. That means that for each $5-item you sell, you make only $0.50. If the minimum payout amount is $100, you will need to sell 200 $5-items to reach your goal. You will need a *massive* amount of traffic to make this number of sales in a month.

High-ticket items on the other hand are those that sell for $100 and up. These items are harder to sell because they require a bigger financial commitment from the consumer. However, you only need a few sales of these items to reach your income goals. If you are selling a $100-item on your website for example, and your commission rate is also 10%, you only need to sell 10 items to earn the minimum payout amount of $100.

It is not wise to make the decision of going for high ticket or low-ticket affiliate programs right now. You will need to consider many factors when making this decision. First, you will need to consider the industry or niche market that you wish to take part in. After that, you will need to consider the types of content that you enjoy creating.

You cannot expect to be successful promoting gadgets and tech-related stuff if your content is all about sports. The product you choose should fit seamlessly with the content you create. They should be aligned with the needs of the visitors of your website. The types of people who visit your website will depend on the content that you have in there and the marketing efforts you put in.

The types of offers available in the market will also limit your options for affiliate products. If you are promoting tangible products, you will always have the option of selling Amazon products through the Amazon Associates program. The majority of products in Amazon are low-ticket. In addition, the commission rate for almost all categories start at 4%. This rate is low in the affiliate marketing industry.

Most people who stick with Amazon however, do so because of the company's reputation and reliability. Most people who go to your website already know what Amazon is and you no longer need to upsell the retailer. On the other hand, if you are selling a product from an unpopular source, you will first need to introduce the retailer, talk about their track record and why your readers should buy from them.

Chapter 2 Quiz

Please refer to Appendix B for the answers to this quiz

1. What do you call inexpensive affiliate products?

    A) Low-Ticket Items
    B) Cheap Affiliates
    C) Clickbait
    D) Affiliate bargain

2. What is one advantage of selling an inexpensive affiliate product?

    A) It has a high commission
    B) It always comes with a high commission rate
    C) It is easy to sell
    D) It requires higher financial commitment for the consumer

3. What is one disadvantage of selling an inexpensive affiliate product?

    A) It does not come with a warranty
    B) It is too easy to sell
    C) You need to pay a lot in advertising fees to promote it
    D) You need to make a lot of sales to reach the payment threshold

4. How do you earn big with this kind of products?

    A) You need to have high quantity of sales
    B) You only need to sell two or three items every week
    C) You need to pay more on advertising
    D) You need to focus your efforts in search marketing

5. What do you call expensive affiliate products?

    A) High-ticket Items
    B) Low-Ticket Items
    C) High rollers
    D) Golden affiliate products

6. What is one advantage of selling an expensive affiliate product?

    A) It comes with a lot of freebies
    B) It can come with a one-year warranty
    C) It is easy to sell

D) You only need to make a few sales to reach the pay out

7. What is one disadvantage of selling an expensive affiliate product?

   A) It is easy to sell
   B) It is faster to sell
   C) It comes with a lot of disclaimers
   D) None of the above

8. Why is it harder to sell this type of item?

   A) It requires higher financial commitment for the consumer
   B) It is difficult to ship
   C) It comes with a high shipping fee
   D) It does not look appealing to the buyer

9. What factor should you consider when choosing between inexpensive and expensive affiliate products?

   A) The need of the consumers
   B) The price of the competitor's products
   C) The reach of your marketing efforts
   D) The state of the world economy

10. What example of low-ticket market was mentioned in the chapter?

    A) Amazon
    B) ClickBank
    C) Shopify
    D) eBay

Inspiration #3

"Don't let the fear of losing be greater than the excitement of winning."

Robert Kiyosaki

Chapter 3:

How To Become An Affiliate Marketer

To become an affiliate marketer, you only need to become a member of a good affiliate marketing program and start spreading the affiliate link. To make money consistently however, you need to be smart in your approach in the business.

Here are the things you will need to start with this business:

A website

As stated in the previous chapters, most affiliate programs require that you have a website before you will be accepted. Advertisers check the website to see what types of content you have. Some advertisers are extremely picky when choosing affiliates. They only accept those whose websites can bring in huge amounts of traffic. Don't worry though, because there are also beginner level affiliate marketing programs that will accept even publishers with new websites.

A profitable niche

You cannot just create any type of website if you want to become a successful affiliate marketer. In particular, you need to be careful in choosing the niche market. We will discuss how you can choose the right niche market in future chapters. For now, just remember that the types of affiliate marketing products that you can sell will depend on the niche market you choose to participate in. If you want to sell only high ticket items for instance, you need to make sure that the niche market you've chosen have high-ticket affiliate marketing programs.

An organic source of traffic

In the world of internet marketing, there are two ways for you to get traffic, organic and paid. While some affiliate marketers do use paid methods to earn through affiliate marketing, these methods exposes you to a higher financial risk. Those who use these methods have developed their skill over years of trial and error.

For now, you should focus on building assets that will help you gather organic visitors. This includes social media accounts and pages, forum memberships, accounts in niche specific online communities, offline traffic sources and other similar assets. You will need to think about where you will get your traffic for your website if you want to be successful from day one.

A membership to an affiliate marketing program

There are tons of affiliate marketing programs in the web. However, not all of them will be suitable to offer to the type of traffic that you can get. You will need to choose an affiliate program that fits the needs of the audience. We will discuss how to choose the best affiliate marketing programs for your audience in the following chapters.

The four factors above are the minimum requirements for becoming a successful affiliate marketer. After choosing an affiliate marketing program, you can apply directly from the web. Most of the application processes just require you to fill up a form with your personal details. In addition, the application form may also ask how you plan to generate traffic for your affiliate offers and what types of products you wish to promote. The form may also ask you how much traffic your own website gets a day and what other monetization methods you use in the said website.

In addition, you may be asked to fill up a tax form. This part will depend on the requirements of the country of origin of the affiliate program. When signing up for Amazon Associates for Amazon.com for instance, US citizens will be asked to fill up a US tax form. A different form will be required if you are applying for Amazon.ca (Canada) Associates program.

How hard is the application process?

For some affiliate programs, getting in is easy. Some may even automatically approve your application. There are more specialized programs though, that will ask for more requirements after you apply. The most demanding programs will have their employees scan your website for the quality of the content. If they are not satisfied with the design or the quality of the content of your website, they may reject your application.

These extremely selective programs usually do this for different reasons. The majority of them do it because they want to protect their brand. Big brands only want to be associated with websites that have good quality content. Some of them will only accept websites that have been around for a long time with hundreds of archived content. Some brands will also reject your application if they see that your website or your contents are not aligned with their target consumers. If your website is in English for example and you apply with an affiliate program for Spanish people, you are likely to be rejected.

My application has been approved, what now?

It is after the application process that the real work begins. Now that you have a product or service to promote, you can now start gathering traffic and funneling them towards your affiliate links. There are multiple methods on how you can do this.

First, you can use paid methods as a source of traffic. You can use advertising platforms that allow affiliate links and pay for the clicks or the views that your ad gets. With this method, you are spending money to make money. You will need a bankroll of hundreds, if not thousands of dollars to make this strategy work. You will also need to make sure that you follow the guidelines set by the affiliate advertisers.

Most of them will restrict you from using certain keywords in the advertising targeting. If you are selling Nike rubber shoes for example, the affiliate program contract may restrict you from using the keywords like Nike. They do this to prevent affiliate marketers from competing with the mother company in the advertising bidding.

The second method of sending traffic is to spread the link around the web. In the past, people used to do sleazy techniques to get clicks on their affiliate links. Some of them for instance, put their affiliate links in the signature part of their forum accounts. This way, when people see their forum comments, they also see the affiliate links. Many forums learned about this technique and now ban the use of links in the signature.

Some affiliate programs also allow the use of redirects and pop-ups to gather traffic. An affiliate marketer using redirect for example, may set up a page that will automatically redirect to the affiliate website. When the visitor visits that page, they are automatically transferred to the affiliate program's landing page. The problem with this strategy is that most people who go through the automatic redirect are sent to the affiliate program's website unwillingly. The majority of them will bounce (i.e. leave rather than continuing to see other pages on the website). This excess traffic of non-buyers will eventually take its toll in the advertiser's website. This is the reason why many affiliate programs ban the use of redirects.

Some people also use link pop-ups to send people through the affiliate link. They may set the pop-up to appear after a certain link in the website is clicked. Upon clicking the said link, another window or tab will open. This works both for desktop and for mobile browsers. When the pop-up opens, the affiliate link is triggered and the affiliate landing page starts to load.

This process of sending traffic to affiliate programs is also problematic. Aside from being prohibited by most affiliate programs, browsers also tend to have pop-up blocking technology. This prevents most of the pop-ups from opening even when the right link is clicked.

The recommended way of gathering traffic for your affiliate programs is through the use of content marketing. Simply put, content marketing is the process of gathering internet user's attention by using different types of content media. One has the option of using text, audio, images, videos or a combination of all these to invite people to go to your website.

News websites are a classic example of websites that use content marketing. They create news articles and accompany them with videos and relevant images. After creating them, they post their content in their social media properties. They spread their news articles through Facebook, Twitter, and other social media marketing platforms. When a person interested in the news sees the article, the headline and the accompanying image should compel them to click on the link of the article. This will lead them to the news website.

After reading the article, they may press the up-vote button for the content. Some may even share a link of the content to their friends. By doing this, they are spreading the news and increasing the reach of the news article. Other people interested in the news may also click on the article. Afterwards they may also share the content with their own social media followers, continuing to spread the news.

Some people who may be looking to read that specific news article may also go to Google and do a search. Because of proper search engine optimization practices, the article landed in the top spot of the search result page with its relevant keywords or key phrases. Because of this, more people from Google manage to read the content. Some of the readers who are interested in the content of the article may also choose to share it with their friends.

While this may seem like a simplistic illustration of how content marketing works, this is how it happens for most content on the web. Content creators simple make the content and share them in the relevant online hotspots. They develop their skill in getting people's attention over thousands of hours of practice.

You could also do the same with your affiliate marketing business. You could lure internet users to go to your website by creating and sharing content that are relevant to their interests and needs. In the process of viewing your content, they should also see the affiliate ads that you share in your website. A percentage of them will click on these marketing materials and make a purchase. You will receive a percentage of the sale amount that your referred customers spend.

Chapter 3 Quiz
Please refer to Appendix C for the answers to this quiz

1. What is the primary marketing asset of the affiliate marketer?

    A) Website
    B) Money
    C) Affiliate program
    D) Friends

2. What do you call a topic that the affiliate website is focusing on?

    A) Preferred topic of interest
    B) Featured Topic
    C) Favorites
    D) Niche Topic

3. Why does a website need marketing?

    A) To send massive amounts of traffic to the advertiser's landing page
    B) To help the website become popular
    C) To increase the chances of winning affiliate promotions
    D) To prevent spammers from infiltrating the affiliate networks

4. How do demanding affiliate programs judge your application?

    A) They ask you to sell them a pen
    B) They email your referrals to check if you are a real person
    C) They use bots to look up your information online
    D) They check your website manually

5. Why are some affiliate programs strict in accepting affiliates?

    A) They are protecting their brands from Spamming marketers
    B) They do not want to accept low-ticket marketers
    C) They do not have enough slots for more marketers
    D) They reserve their slots only for high-ticket marketers

6. What are the two general ways of sending traffic to your affiliate website?

    A) Paid and Free
    B) Social and Search
    C) Email and Search

D) Ads and Search traffic

7. What do you call the strategy of using content to attract traffic to a website?

    A) Search Marketing
    B) Content Marketing
    C) Social Media Marketing
    D) Banner Marketing

8. Where is content marketing most effective?

    A) Social networks
    B) Email Marketing
    C) Offline Marketing
    D) Banner Marketing

9. What do you call the process of making your content rank well in search engine result pages?

    A) Social Engine Marketing
    B) Search Engine Optimization
    C) Search Media Optimization
    D) Traffic Source

10. What is an example of a type website that uses content marketing routinely?

    A) Software support website
    B) Purely Ecommerce website
    C) Membership website
    D) News Website

Inspiration #4

"If you can dream it, you can do it."

Walt Disney

Chapter 4

The Top 20 Affiliate Marketing Programs

There are hundreds of affiliate marketing programs to choose from. However, to become successful, you need to find the one with the best potential for earning. You need to consider many factors such as the stability of the company running the network. You should also consider what types of advertisers and products they have in their network. In this chapter we will discuss some of the biggest affiliate programs right now.

1. Amazon Associates

Amazon is probably the most commonly used program by beginners. It allows you to earn from any type of item sold in Amazon, aside from digital kindle products. The program though, covers all tangible products. The commission rate varies for each product, depending on the type of product your associates account sells. Most items start out at 4% for the first six sales of the month. The rate for the seventh until the 30th item on the other hand is 6%. The rate increases as the number of products you sell also increases. In this affiliate program, affiliates are rewarded for selling a high quantity of items. The more items you sell in a month, the higher your commission rate will be.

Unlike most affiliate marketing programs, Amazon does not have a fixed landing page for their products. They allow the affiliate marketer to choose a product and use the product page as the landing page.

The best part about selling through Amazon Associates is that the affiliate marketer will be credited for any item bought by a person that clicked their link. The person you referred to Amazon does not need to buy the product you suggested. As long as they clicked your link, you will receive commission for everything that they buy in the website.

A person who clicks your regular Amazon Associates link has 24 hours to make a purchase for it to be credited to your account. If they do not make a purchase after 24 hours, the cookie will expire. Any purchase they make after the cookie expires will no longer be credited to you.

A special type of link that you can generate in your Amazon Associates account automatically leads to the clicker's cart page after they log in to their Amazon account. If you use this kind of affiliate link, the affiliate cookie extends to 90 days. As long as the item is kept in their cart in the 90-day period, you will be credited for the sale. In addition, if the person buys other things from Amazon in addition to the item in their cart, the sale of these items will also be credited to you.

Apart from the lower commission rates based on the industry standards, the only downside with selling through Amazon is that it will not redirect the Amazon links for you based on the visitor's location.

2. CJ.com

CJ or Commission Junction is one of the longest running affiliate network in the world. CJ is an affiliate network that connects affiliate marketers with advertisers. After signing up to CJ.com, you will be able to apply to the different advertisers they have in the website. Some of the advertisers allow immediate approval of applications. Others however, will manually check the application and may reject it depending on their acceptance standards.

CJ.com provides the tools that you will need for setting up the affiliate links in your website. They will also provide you with a dashboard where you can check how many clicks your affiliate marketing efforts get. This is also the place where you will see the amount you earn from the clicks you get.

The links that you will get from your CJ.com console will go straight to the advertiser's landing page. It is important that you choose the landing pages that you use. Choose a landing page, that you think will have a high chance of converting visits into sales.

The commission rates for affiliate programs in CJ vary per advertiser. This rate is usually written in the description of the program. While Amazon Associates rates are capped at 7.5%, it is normal for some advertisers in CJ.com to offer 10%. If you prove that you can send a good quantity of high quality leads, you may even request the advertiser for a higher commission rate.

3. Clickbank

Clickbank is also popular among affiliate marketers, mainly for its high commission rates. They sell a variety of products and services, from arts and entertainment to travel and leisure. Just go to their website at clickbank.com and go to the Affiliate Marketplace. In this page, you will see the different categories of affiliate offers that they have. Upon clicking on one of these categories, you will see a list of products and services. After choose a product or service that you would like to promote, you will need to sign up to the program by clicking the "Promote" button.

Most of clickbank's affiliate advertisers sell digital product and online services. Because of this, they can offer extremely high commission rates. Some of them offer up to 70% of the price of the purchase. These types of rate are only possible with online products and services. Because of the high commission rates, affiliate marketers prefer to promote clickbank content.

4. Rakuten Linkshare

Rakuten Linkshare is also one of the most popular affiliate programs. The sign up process for this program is fairly simple. You only need to fill up the usual information fields as well as complete the tax form. After which, your account will be registered and you will be allowed to sign up.

Once logged in, you will be able to select a category of products. The number of products available in Rakuten Linkshare is significantly fewer compared to the other affiliate networks discussed above. However, Linkshare has the reputation of being reliable for fast payments for both US and non-US based affiliates.

5. JVZoo

JVZoo is new to the market but it is one of the fastest growing affiliate program in the industry. It offers features that are not commonly found in other affiliate programs. For instance, they are the only program that commits to timely payment delivery. This is a common issue among many programs. It usually takes them time to validate sales reports to make sure there are no sales frauds in the records. Some of the longest running programs like CJ.com and ClickBank still take weeks and even months to deliver payments for members with large volumes of sales.

6. Avantlink

Avantlink is less popular than the first few programs we've discussed above. However, its wide range of advertiser categories and its beginner-friendly user interface also makes it a great affiliate network.

7. eBay

EBay tends to be forgotten in the affiliate marketing world because of its strict approval process. Because eBay does not sell its own products and does not take responsibility in the quality of their products, affiliates tend to avoid promoting products from there. It's brand however, makes the network an easy sell to the average shopper. The shop is particularly popular among bargain hunters. If your website attracts of bargain hunters, eBay affiliate may work for you.

8. Shareasale

Shareasale's competitive edge is the size of its network. It offers more than 4,000 advertisers in various categories. Its user interface is also easy to use and it collects some types of analytics data not available in other networks. It is also one of those networks that pay on a monthly basis.

9. Avangate

Avangate exclusively offers affiliate offers from software. They offer the best brands in software downloads and online services. As with other technology-based affiliate programs, Avantgate advertisers tend to offer higher commission rates.

10. Affibank

Affibank.com is also a newer player in the market but they are making a name for themselves among affiliate marketers because of their high commission rates. Many of the offers in the Affibank give out commission rates of 75%. This means that a big chunk of the money you refer goes back to you. The offers in this marketplace are similar to those found in ClickBank. The only downside is that they are currently offering few offers and most of them are in the Health, Beauty and Fitness Categories.

There are hundreds of other affiliate marketing programs available for you to explore. Here are ten more that you can look into if you cannot find a program you like in the marketplaces listed above.

11. Maxbounty

12. RevenueWire

13. ReviMedia

14. Flexoffers

15. Commission Factory

16. PeerFly

17. ClickFunnels

18. Tradedoubler

19. AffiliateWindow

20. BankAffiliates

While these marketplaces are the best places to start, you can also look into in-house affiliate programs in specific companies. Some online companies maintain their own affiliate marketing programs. If you have a company whose products you wish to promote, you can search their company with the key phrase "affiliate program" added to it.

If they do have an affiliate program, there is no doubt that it will show up in the search result pages. Think of the products and services that you have been using in the past and check online if they do have an affiliate marketing program set up. One example is Shopify. You can promote it to people who want to start an online store and earn while doing it.

Chapter 4 Quiz
Please refer to Appendix D for the answers to this quiz

1. What types of products can you sell with Amazon Associates

    A) All tangible products sold in Amazon.com
    B) All products in Amazon.com and eBay.com
    C) Products in Amazon.com, Amazon.au and Shopify
    D) All digital products in Amazon.com

2. What affiliate program consistently offers high commission rates

    A) CJ.com
    B) Affibank
    C) Amazon Associates
    D) eBay

3. Why is Shareasale a strong network?

    A) It has lots of advertisers and offers
    B) It has a strong social media following
    C) It is recommended by celebrities
    D) It offers a high commission rates

4. What is JVZoo's defining feature?

    A) High number of offers
    B) Fast payment processing
    C) Longest running affiliate network
    D) Multinational reach

5. What type of products does a Avantgate offer?

    A) Sports equipment
    B) Software
    C) Computer Hardware
    D) Cars

6. What is eBay's best feature?

    A) Brand recognition
    B) Product quality
    C) Business process

D) Superior customer service

7. What is Amazon Associate's best feature?

A) High commission rate
E) High volume of products
F) Superior customer service
G) Fast payment processing

8. What is CJ.com's best feature?

A) High commission rate
B) High number of advertisers
C) Superior customer service
D) Fast payment processing

9. What is an example of a company that offers in-house affiliate program

A) Shopify
B) Nike
C) Under Armour
D) ESPN

10. What do you call a company that hosts its own affiliate program without passing through a network?

A) Affiliate network guru
B) Business process outsourcing
C) Virtual Assistants
D) In-house affiliate program

Inspiration #5

"Many of life's failures are people who did not realize how close they were to success when they gave up."

Thomas Edison

Chapter 5:

How To Choose An Affiliate Marketing Program

Choosing an affiliate marketing program is an important factor in becoming a successful affiliate marketer. If you choose the wrong program, you may end up not making any money from all your efforts. You need to align the content you created with the right types of products in the affiliate marketing program. You also need to make sure that the commission rate in the program you've chosen is big enough. Lastly, you need to make sure that the company behind the program provides excellent customer support and fast payment processing.

Check the advertisers

The advertisers should be the primary reason why you should join an affiliate program. If you find an advertiser you like in an affiliate network, you should join that network. Not all advertisers you would like to partner with will all be in one program. To be able to sell all the products and services that you personally like, you may need to work with multiple advertisers. This means that you will need to work with multiple affiliate accounts.

Find the programs with the best commission rate

Aside from the types of advertisers they have, you should also join programs based on their commission rates. The commission rate of a program varies depending on the type of product sold. Usually, the commission rate goes up when the product is digital (such as in the case of software) or when the product is hard to sell. Companies that are having a hard time selling their product tend to add a high commission rate to their product to increase the motivation of online marketers to sell them.

You should also watch out for the types of products that also offer residual payments. In affiliate marketing, residual payments happen when the people you refer to the program renew their membership in a merchant. This type of payment usually applies towards services that require customers to become members. Many web hosting affiliate programs for example, offer this kind of deal to people. With this type of commission payment, you will continue to make money from people that you referred even years ago.

Based on the quality of backend services

Lastly, you need to consider the quality of service of the affiliate program. Most affiliate programs tend to offer a do-it-yourself approach to marketing. However, they do offer one-on-one support when the affiliates need help with technical parts of the website. Choosing a company that has good customer support is important so that there will be someone to help you in the future when problems in your account arise. Whenever you find a new program that looks promising, look into the reputation of its customer service online.

If the company has a poor customer service, you will hear about it in the forums and blog posts. Check other people's experiences about how fast the company responds to queries and reports. More importantly, you should also research on how fast the company delivers payments and what types of payment methods they use.

Chapter 5 Quiz
Please refer to Appendix E for the answers to this quiz

1. What should be the primary reason for joining an affiliate program?

    A) The advertiser
    B) The competition
    C) The email marketing service
    D) None of the above

2. What determines the amount paid to the advertiser?

    A) Success rate
    B) Commission rate
    C) Popularity of the product
    D) Customer service

3. What do you do if the advertisers you want are in different affiliate networks?

    A) Apply in both networks
    B) Abandon one network over the other
    C) Find an alternative advertiser in your preferred network
    D) Create to websites to promote different products

4. What is a common problem among affiliate programs?

    A) High bounce rates
    B) Slow internet connection
    C) Slow payment processing
    D) Spam marketing content

5. What usually determines the commission rate of the program?

    A) The popularity of product
    B) The type of product sold
    C) The number of annual sales
    D) The popularity of the website

6. What do you do when you encounter a technical issue with your affiliate program?

    A) Transfer to another affiliate program
    B) Replace all your affiliate links with working ones
    C) Contact the affiliate program support group

D) Wait for the problem to be solved on its own

7. What makes a good affiliate program support team?

    A) Making excuses for not solving problems
    E) Presence of email support
    F) Fast and accurate responses from the team
    G) Great reviews from online bloggers

8. How do you check if the affiliate program support group is any good?

    A) If they are available in multiple communication channels
    B) If they are good at upselling products from the affiliate program
    C) If they are available during business hours only
    D) If do not respond through emails

9. How do you make sure that an affiliate program pays?

    A) Find program reviews in YouTube and in personal blogs
    B) Wait until you reach the payment threshold
    C) You cannot have any guarantees
    D) Buy the affiliate products yourself to reach the payment threshold

10. From a payment standpoint, what should you check before you apply with an affiliate program of network?

    A) The past earnings of other people
    B) The total revenue of the affiliate advertiser
    C) The methods of payment offered by the program or network
    D) The cost of contacting the affiliate support team

Inspiration #6

"The secret of success is to do the common thing uncommonly well."

John D. Rockefeller Jr.

Chapter 6:

Writing Content For Affiliate Marketing

To start your content marketing campaign, you should begin with the product or products that you wish to promote to your visitors.

Promote products you've used in the past

Ideally, you should share products that you have used in the past, so that you can share your firsthand experience in using them. This will make your content authentic. Online authorities usually use this kind of approach. A welding teacher for example, uses his website together with YouTube to create a multimedia content experience. In his articles and videos, he shows people how to do welding techniques and projects. In the process, he shows them the tools that he is using. By showing the people that he is using the tools, he is more likely to convince them to buy from his affiliate marketing sources.

If you choose to present yourself and your website as an authority in the subject you are using, you can also use this strategy. When thinking about the topic that you are going to discuss, also research on the possible products that you may promote to your online visitors. It's better if you already have some of these products so that you no longer need to buy them.

Presenting products you haven't used

Some affiliate marketers in the market also suggest the use of products they have never used in the past. This type of affiliate marketing suggestion usually works for generic products that people will still buy regardless of the price or the brand you present. Weight plates for dumbbells are an example of this type of product. Even if you do not show that you are using weight plates, you can talk about them, show photos of them and present an affiliate link for them.

Because they are common products, your readers are familiar with what these products are. They will also be willing to buy them even if you do not show yourself using them. If you post a link to an Amazon product page with an acceptable price range, some of your uses will make the purchase.

When presenting products that you haven't used yet, you should do all the research you can about it. The web today is rich in information, you can do your research about any product out there. If the product can be found in Amazon, you can even use the review section as your source for doing product research. The people posting these reviews mostly have firsthand experience in using them.

Beginners make the common mistake of being too positive about the products they present. This makes them sound as if they are doing a sales pitch; you do not want people to see you this way when you are talking about your content. Instead, people want hard facts about the products you are presenting. Show them both the pros and cons of using the product.

What type of content should I create?

When choosing the type of content you will create, choose the ones where in you can actively and naturally suggest the products you use. Listicles (list articles), tutorial articles and tips articles are some of the types of contents where in you can naturally plug a product in. Ideally, you should create three types of content. An article in your website for people who prefer to read, a video in YouTube and an audio version of the video for iTunes. You can embed the video and audio files in your article page to make all your content come together.

In addition, you can also create additional content such as behind-the-scenes videos and photos. You can then post these photos in your social media accounts or your website blog. By doing so, you will be able to keep your accounts active. Some of the people who see your social media content will also be interested in what you are up to. If you show a photo doing a project for example, your followers may become interested in knowing what project you are working on.

By posting these behind-the-scenes footage and content, you will be able to build excitement in your audience base. This increases the potential views of your different contents from the different platforms you use.

All these pieces of content have one important purpose, to redirect the attention of the visitor towards the affiliate links and buttons. Your target market will be minding their own business, using social media or doing a Google search. In the process, they may stumble upon your content and spend some time to watch, read or listen to it. This is what you are fighting for when doing content marketing, your potential visitors' time and attention. You want to keep them tuned in to your content long enough so that they will see or hear your product pitches.

Putting the Tips into Action

Now that you know how the basic content marketing process works, let's consider an example of a successful content marketing campaign for an affiliate marketing program.

Mary is a stay at home mom and she wants to start doing affiliate marketing to supplement the household income. In her free time, Mary likes to work on her garden and she has had some success in growing both flowering and fruit-bearing plants. Because she enjoys gardening and she has the experience to teach people how to do it, she decided that this will be her niche topic.

Mary begins by researching about the types of information that are already in the market. As she expected, there are already a lot of content about general gardening. Because of this, she decided to make her niche narrower. She looked into creating content only for specific aspects of gardening such as organic gardening, composting, and similar contents. She found that while there are already a lot of content in this area, she has some article ideas that no other website have discussed with depth.

With her niche market set, Mary begins to craft her content marketing strategy. In the beginning of the website, there will not be a lot of traffic because people will not be aware yet that the website exists. This gives Mary the opportunity to create and refine her content. She starts by creating a series of posts focused on planting lettuce in her backyard. She did her research and outlined her content so that everything will be organized and easy to follow.

While researching, she also followed the tip of listing down all the tools she will need for her series of articles. In her list, she included both generic garden tools and some brands that she personally uses. After creating the list, she looks for these products in Amazon and uses her Amazon Associates account to generate links for each one of them.

Now that the information for the content is ready, Mary starts to create. To create her content, she works on her garden and uses her smartphone camera to take photos and to record videos. She plans to edit these videos and share them in YouTube. She also takes photos and short videos and shares them in Instagram, Pinterest, Twitter and Facebook. In the process, some of her friends start interacting with her content, asking her what she is up to. She lets them know that she is working on her garden and creating an article about it. With her initial social media content, starts to pique the interest of her natural audience.

After her gardening project, she managed to create 5 articles about plating lettuce, one video about how to plant them from seeds and multiple social media posts about it. These become her first contents for her website and her YouTube Channel. In both her articles and her YouTube video, she actively discusses the tools and planting products she uses. She then tells her content viewers that they can also get the same products through the link she provides. In her articles, she posts the link directly after mentioning them. In her YouTube video, she puts all her affiliate links in the description of the video. She also includes a link towards her articles so that people from YouTube will be able to go to her website easily.

Now that her first set of contents are ready, Mary begins the second part of her content marketing effort. She now starts to spread her content around the web. She continues to post in her social media platforms about the progress of the growth of her plants. In Instagram she posts photos of the sprouts coming out of the ground, she also posts about the different plants in her garden.

She also shares the same content in her Twitter account. In there, she also talks with other Twitter users about gardening. Every now and then, she mentions her articles and her videos. In Facebook, Mary posts her articles and uploads a copy of her video. In the beginning, only her friends and family talked about it. Mary entertained her audience in the comments. With people engaged in her articles and her video, the reach of her content increases. Because of this, other people outside of Mary's social circles start seeing her contents. They press the up-vote button while some leave a comment and share the content.

Aside from social media marketing, Mary also optimizes her content so that it ranks high in search engine result pages. She uses her target keywords in the title of her content as well as in different paragraphs in the article. In her YouTube video, she also created a long description with the relevant keywords included to make it easier to find for people looking for videos.

All these marketing efforts increased the views of Mary's articles and video. Out of the thousands that viewed her content, some clicked on the Amazon links she provided. The purchases of these referred visitors allowed Mary to earn some cash from Amazon Associates.

In this example, our protagonist did all things right to make money through Amazon. Here are some of the content marketing best practices she did right:

Pick a topic you enjoy working on

You are stuck with the topic you pick until you see success or until you give up on your affiliate marketing business. To make sure you do not get fed up making content on the same topics, you should pick one that you love doing, in our example, Mary chose to work on gardening, one of her natural interests. If you have a long-term interest or hobby, you can also pick that topic for your content marketing.

Create specific types of content based on your marketing platform

Right now, the Google and Facebook are the two biggest sources of website visitors. They are so influential that they are rumored to be used for important political events like elections. While they are both excellent places to share content, not all types of content will work in both of them. For Google, it's best to use keyword-rich instructional contents. People go to Google when they have problems or when they are looking for specific information.

For Facebook on the other hand, the best types of content are those that provoke certain emotions on the readers. They do not need to be necessarily useful. In fact, many of the contents in Facebook are purely for entertainment purposes. Content in Facebook become popular if people engage with it. Engagement in social media marketing is defined as any positive action done by the user towards the content. In Facebook, reactions such as "Likes" are examples of engagement. Comments and Shares are even more powerful forms of engagement. The Facebook content management algorithm will show your content to more people if it received a lot of these positive reactions in the first hour of posting.

Encourage followers to engage with your content

In our example, Mary knew that engagement is important in her content marketing game. Because of this, she entertained the comments of people in the content she shared. The more comments and reactions the content gets, the higher the number of people that gets to see it.

You should also do the same when doing content marketing is social networks. Make your content rise in the newsfeeds of your friends and family by entertaining comments. Also encourage people to share the content by directly asking them to do it in the content description.

State a clear call-to-action to go to the affiliate website

People will not just click on your affiliate link just because you added it to your content. They will only click on it if you directly invite them to do so. In our example, Mary directly invites her viewers and website visitors to click on the affiliate links she provides. Even better, she shows people that she is using the affiliate products she invites them to buy. Affiliate marketing is more than just a selling business. It's about helping your community solve their own problems. You can only earn if you convince people that your way of solving the problem is better.

Do not be afraid to over use your call-to-action statements and buttons. The business is all about directing the attention of your audience towards your links. If you are shy with making people click on that affiliate link, you will fail in achieving your goal. If you believe that the product you are selling will solve the problems of the people viewing your content, you should not be afraid of sounding to salesy.

Chapter 6 Quiz
Please refer to Appendix F for the answers to this quiz

1. Ideally, which type of product should you promote?

   A) Products that other bloggers are promoting
   B) Products with high ratings on Amazon
   C) Products you have used in the past
   D) Products that look great

2. Why should you promote products you've used in the past?

   A) To increase your credibility as a reviewer and product ambassador
   B) So that it is easy to find out what qualities to upsell
   C) To make it easier to fool consumers
   D) To sell more products

3. What makes a good content in promoting products and services?

   A) Showing people that you use the product
   B) Showing stock photos of the product
   C) Writing only positive qualities of the product
   D) Showing that the product is on sale

4. How do you present yourself and your website as a content authority?

   A) Make up information about your achievements
   B) Show content on how to use a product
   C) Talk about how good you are in your niche topic
   D) Build a visually appealing website about the topic

5. What is the best way to find information about products you've never used before?

   A) Copy content of other affiliate marketers about it
   B) Make things up about the product
   C) Buy the product yourself to test it
   D) Use the information written in the marketing flyers of the product

6. Which of the following is a good source of user information about the product?

   A) It's website
   B) Other blogs
   C) Amazon's review section

D) Magazines

7. What type of content would probably do well in Facebook?

   A) A link post to your latest content
   B) An emotional video related to your content
   C) An image of your website's front page
   D) A rant about your competitors

8. How do you make sure that your content does well in social media?

   A) Post your content in other people's pages
   B) Buy social media up-votes
   C) Create a specific type of content for your chosen social media platform
   D) Post your content in as many groups as possible

9. How do you encourage users to engage with your content?

   A) Put more videos in your content
   B) Entertain people's comments in the website
   C) Talk about how good your content is
   D) Make a pop up that forces people to make a comment

10. How do you convince people to click on your affiliate link?

   A) Fool the user to thinking that he is going to a different website by clicking the link
   B) Fill your webpage with affiliate links
   C) Rant about how bad other products in the market are
   D) State a clear call-to-action to click on the link

Inspiration #7

"The only place where success comes before work is in the dictionary."
Vidal Sassoon

Chapter 7

Using Social Media Platforms For Affiliate Marketing

As mentioned above, social media is one of the best sources of traffic right now. Next to Google search, social media apps will probably become your best source of traffic. Learning how to funnel traffic from these sources can lead to a significant increase in your earnings. To learn how to make use of the different apps in the market, use the following steps:

1. Find the social media website or app where most of your target audience spend their time

There are hundreds of social media apps out there. However, you do not have to participate in all of them. Instead, you only need to find the online communities where most of your target audience hangs out. If you are targeting adults between the ages of 25 and 40, Facebook, Pinterest, Twitter and LinkedIn may be the best options for you. For young adults between 20 and 25, Instagram and Snapchat are the more popular options.

There are more social media options available depending on your target country and the interests of your audience. If you can clearly define what demographics your target audience belongs to, you will be able to choose the right network.

2. Identify what content to share in each network

Each social network favors different types of content. You want to know what type of content each social network requires before you start your social media marketing campaigns.

Facebook is a truly multimedia social networking platform, in that you can post any type of content in there. However, since the time video content was allowed, it has dominated all other types of contents in terms of engagement and reach. You will still need to mix it up though by posting images, text content and links from time to time to add variety to your page.

Instagram on the other hand is focused on hosting images and short videos. Pinterest is used as a tool to collect images from around the web. If you have a project for example, you can use your Pinterest account as a vision board of inspirations.

LinkedIn is just like Facebook. However, the users in this network prefer content that are related to careers, professional networking, finance and personal growth. If you post so-called viral content in LinkedIn, most users will unfollow you. They just do not want their feeds to be filled with distractions.

Twitter is ruled by short text content. You will also find some pictures and videos in there but text conversations dominate this network. You can post your opinions and your thoughts in twitter as long as you make your message fit in the character number limit of the network. You can also react to other people's tweets by pressing or tapping on the heart icon under each tweet. The retweet option however, is the primary sharing feature for tweets. The most popular tweets in the worlds are retweeted millions of times.

Businesses are fond of twitter because they can use it to communicate directly with their fans. It works both as a customer service and a marketing platform.

3. Find out how content is spread in the network

Each social network has a unique way of spreading content. Most social networks use a system where in users can follow other users. When a user follows you, they will see every public post you share in your account. This system is used in almost all the popular social networks today such as Facebook, Twitter, Instagram and Snapchat.

A user with millions of follower is considered an influencer or authority. They hold a lot of power in the social network because any of their posts can be seen by millions of people. As an affiliate marketer, you want your social network accounts to reach this kind of status. You can do this by sharing excellent quality posts.

Aside from increasing the number of followers, you can also share your content by encouraging engagement. This is a second feature common to all social networks. They allow users to engage with content. In Facebook for example, the network allows the users to select a reaction for the content shares. The thumbs-up icon is called the like button.

This is a form of an up-vote towards the content. In recent years, Facebook also added other reactions to convey the user's emotion towards the content. A person who finds the content funny for example, can choose a laughing emoji. If the content is sad, the user also has the option to use the sad emoji. All these reactions however, count as a form of engagement. The more reactions a content gets, the higher the likelihood will be that the content will spread.

Aside from reactions, Facebook can also leave a comment below the content. Facebook comments are powerful engagement signals because sometimes, they encourage other users to also engage in the discussion. The tagging feature of Facebook also helps content spread wider through the comment feature.

In Facebook, the newsfeed is the primary sharing feature among users. When a user shares something on Facebook, that user's followers will see the shared content in their newsfeeds. As an affiliate marketer, you want your shared content to show in the newsfeeds of your target audience. Driving the engagement up in your contents will help you achieve this. More people will discover your content if other users are engaged with the content.

Instagram also has an up-vote feature in the form of a heart. By double tapping an image in Instagram, you are able to up-vote a content. Just like Facebook, Instagram also allows users to comment and to tag other users. While Instagram also has feeds that shows the shared content of the users you follow, this is not how other people will discover your Instagram account.

Most of the content discovery happens in the search screen of the app. When the user taps on the magnifying glass icon in the bottom of the app, the search screen will show. In this part of the app, the user can search for accounts, hashtags, and places. In the same part of the app, they will also see suggested images and video content. The suggestions in this part of the app are based on the perceived interests of the said user. This perceived interest is based on many factors like the accounts followed by the user, the types of images and videos they clicked on or up-voted in the past and past searches made by the user.

For your content to be shown to the right people on Instagram, you should establish your accounts identity. You can do this by controlling the types of content your share. If your Instagram account is about gardening, you should post mostly images and videos about your garden. You can also post about significant events, but you should still increase the frequency of posting content related to your affiliate marketing topic.

You could also establish what your content is about by putting a detailed description of your account in the account Bio. This is the part just below you profile picture and your name when you are looking at your profile page. To make your content spread, you should also add descriptions below your content that are relevant to your affiliate marketing topic. Your content will also reach many other users if you include the right hashtags to it.

Twitter also uses many of the social networking features discussed above. Users in this network can follow one another to subscribe to each other's tweets. However, one does not need to be a follower to participate in the public conversations of other people. Just like with Instagram, people use the search feature to find content here. They can also find related tweets by clicking on hashtags.

Twitter is well known for its high click-through rate. Users in this network are more open to clicking on links. If many of your target audience are twitter users, you may have the opportunity to earn big.

4. Completely create your account and start sharing

If you do not know where to start in using social media, start by choosing a platform where most of your users are found and create an account there. To be successful, you will need to complete all the details of your account. In most cases, you will be required to add a profile image and a larger cover photo in the case of Facebook, Twitter and LinkedIn.

You will also be asked to write a description about yourself or your page. Just fill in whatever form the account creation process gives you.

After creating the account, you should plan how and where you will get your content. It is possible to grow your social media accounts by using other people's images and videos. However, you will find more success if you have an option to create your own content.

5. Facebook and LinkedIn groups

One of the best ways of using social media to keep your audience tuned into the content you create is by using the group feature of social networks. Networks like Facebook and LinkedIn have features that allow you to create groups where network users can join. These groups are effective in keeping your audience engaged with the content you are promoting.

A gardening blog owner from Canada for example, can create a group in Facebook about the topic for his home town. He could then ask his friends and relatives who are interested in gardening to join the group. In the group, he could create conversation topics regularly. An active group can have hundreds to thousands of new content per day. What matters most however, is not the actual number of posts but the amount of engagement of the group members in those posts. Among the different ways to engage in post, comments are probably the biggest newsfeed ranking indicator. The more comments your content gets, the greater its reach will be.

There are two steps to social media group marketing. The first step is the process of growing the group. You can start building the group by talking adding the people you actually know to the group. If you know for sure that a person you know is interested in your affiliate marketing niche, talk to them about it and ask them if they want to join your group.

After tapping your natural circles, you can start using your other marketing tools to promote your group. You can begin by talking about it in every other post in your website. You could then leave a link to your group. You could also promote your group in your different social media accounts. If you have a Facebook page, you should link it to your group.

The easiest way to increase the number of member of your group is by introducing it to the people you meet every day who are also interested in the niche topic. If you meet a coworker for example who also likes your content, you could tell them about your group. This group is an effective way for you to create a place for all your followers to meet each other. Your follower can be from different social networks and some may even find you on Facebook. By having a group in Facebook or LinkedIn, you will have a place where they can all meet and have a conversation amongst themselves.

If you are not familiar with how social media groups work, you could begin by joining one first. Ideally, you should join one that is related to your chosen affiliate marketing niche. Observe how the manager or administrators of the group keep the users engaged. Take note of the types of content that he or she is posting in the group. The purpose of these groups is for people to have meaningful conversations about the common topic that they are interested in. However, it could also be for other purposes. Sometimes, people use these groups to build relationships. Others do it to solve problems. They do this by posting a question in the group, hoping that group members will be able to answer it.

While you are in the group, start participating in the conversation. If you see a question that you know the answer to, answer it for the person asking. Also, while you are there, observe how different types of content rise up in the groups newsfeeds. Just like in any other type of social media newsfeeds, the content in social media groups are usually shown based on the amount of engagement they get. In short, contents with a lot of comments and reactions tend to be shown to more viewers.

Also, take note of how the members interact and how they react to posts. In places like Facebook, you are more likely to see people talking in a casual manner, sometimes even using informal writing to communicate. In LinkedIn, people tend to communicate in a more respectful and politically correct way. You will need to set the tone with how people communicate in your own group in the future.

The group will only continue to grow beyond the people you add if the community becomes active. To do this, you could make the group come alive by keeping the conversations going. You could do this by sharing content to it. You may also appoint some of the most active members of the group to become your co-administrators. These people will help you police the group and to make it a pleasant place for the members. They can also help in keeping the community members active. You should not worry if the progress of growing your group seems slow. As long as you keep adding content and keep participating in your own group, it will continue to grow.

The content that you share in the group does not have to be always your own. You could put content from other sources as well, as long as they fit the purpose of the group. Every time you post a new content in your website however, be sure to post it in the group.

If the group grows, you can even use it as a way to drive some affiliate sales. The members of a group about professional networking for instance, will be interested in new books about the topic. If the group owner sees an interesting book, he could make a post about it in his book. He could then use Amazon Associate links to promote the book in the group. If some of the group members buy from Amazon after using the link, you may earn commission from it.

Congratulations!

The fourth character of the password required to unlock the Traffic Optimization Secrets booklet is letter a.

Chapter 7 Quiz
Please refer to Appendix G for the answers to this quiz

1. Which of the following statements is true?

   A) You should create accounts in all social networking websites and apps
   B) You only need to learn how to use Facebook
   C) Instagram is the best app to use right now
   D) The choice for the best social media platform to use depends on your target audience

2. From a marketing standpoint, what is the most important aspect of a social networking app or website?

   A) The visually appealing content
   B) The underlying technology
   C) The community of likeminded individuals
   D) The ease of entry to the app

3. What is the best way to communicate your website to social media users

   A) Communicate with the social media users in a natural but charismatic way
   B) Flood your account with promotional content
   C) Pay other users to do the marketing for you
   D) Attack the beliefs of others users to gain attention from the rest of the community

4. Which social network should you use if you have a great video content to share?

   A) Instagram
   B) Twitter
   C) LinkedIn
   D) It depends on the topic of the video

5. Which social network is great for promoting products for professionals?

   A) Instagram
   B) Twitter
   C) Pinterest
   D) LinkedIn

6. How does content spread in Facebook?

   A) People share them
   B) They naturally spread through newsfeed algorithm
   C) They only spread through ads

D) Only private contents are allowed in Facebook

7. Which of the following has a high impact in the spread of content in Social Media?

   A) Mention of brand names and celebrities
   B) Time of posting
   C) Hashtags
   D) Engagement with the content

8. What feature of Facebook allows people of the same interest to meet?

   A) Facebook Live
   B) Facebook groups
   C) Newsfeeds
   D) Messenger

9. What feature in groups will have the biggest impact in helping the spread of content?

   A) Likes
   B) Comments
   C) Spam
   D) Pinning of content

10. What is the best part of having a successful social media group?

    A) Being liked by the members of the group
    B) Being popular in the social network
    C) Instant likes in your posts
    D) Access to a homogenous audience

Inspiration #8

"Success is not final; failure is not fatal: It is the courage to continue that counts."

Winston S. Churchill

Chapter 8

Common Affiliate Marketing Mistakes

Many people who try to build an affiliate marketing business fail because they make common mistakes that end up ruining their business. In this section, we will discuss the most important mistakes so that you will be able to avoid them when you do start your own affiliate marketing career.

1. Thinking that a website is the only way to sell affiliate products

Many affiliate marketers make the mistake of focusing too much on their website and not finding other opportunities outside to promote their affiliate products. Every now and then, your followers will forgive you if you promote to them through Facebook, Twitter or even Instagram.

When guest posting in your friends' website, you can also post affiliate links relevant to your topic. Make sure that you get the permission of the website owner first. Few will actually allow you to do so. However, if it is possible, you should take the opportunity.

2. Not building a community from day one

The biggest affiliate marketers in the industry can demand certain discounts, freebies and other promotions. They can do this because tens to hundreds of thousands of people follow their content. This is your goal and it makes sense to start building this goal for day one.

From your first article or video, you should already start considering your audience as a part of that community. If you have this kind of mindset, you will be able to avoid making some of the basic mistakes in this list. With a community building mindset, you will put your community member's interest first. You will not focus on factors like commission rates of your products or conversion rates of your marketing tools. Instead, you will be able to focus on helping the members of your community. You can do this by providing useful content to your audience (community members) and opening them to exclusive offers that only you can give them.

In the beginning though, try to help your community members by providing them with the information they need. As your community grows, you will be repaid by the love they show your content. They will talk about it, not only in the comment areas of your website but also in other places online.

3. Becoming too salesy by claiming exaggerated results

Many affiliate marketers think that selling is all about highlighting the positive parts of the products they promote. This is far from what is actually happening in reality. The population of internet users is becoming smarter each year. They are becoming more mindful of false information. This is especially true with internet buyers. With thousands of products available online, the average consumer have options on where to get their products.

If you make exaggerated claims regarding the features and benefits of the product you are promoting, most people will call you out for it. People are more vigilant now with these types of schemes. If they think that you are fooling people with your claims, they may make a post about it in social media. It is common nowadays for regular people to attack business by posting negative things about them online.

When posting about your products in any of your content, you should make it a habit only to talk about the facts. When using a product for instance, you should only talk about how you like to personally use it. Talk about the pros and cons of the product based on your experience. If you set an extremely high expectation, your audience will be disappointed when the product actually arrives in the mail. Because you have a website, they will be able to go back to your claims and leave negative comments. They may even call your entire business a scam. You do not want this to happen to you.

4. Not working with a partner

An affiliate marketing business is easy to start. You can definitely fund it and work on it on your own. However, it is also the ease of entry that makes it easy to let go. Many of people who fail at affiliate marketing give up on the task before they even start making money. When they fail to see results in the first few weeks of creating content, they start to doubt the process and consider quitting. Many of them give up on their project before the sixth month period.

One way to avoid this is by working with others who believe in your vision. I am not talking about hiring an employee. Instead, I am talking about working with a partner. A business partner motivates you to work on the business even when you do not want to. It also has the same effect on your partner. They will also be forced to work on the business because you are holding them accountable.

A partner not only increases the amount of work hours put on a business but also gives it a longer financial runway. In startups, the runway refers to amount of time that the capital fund of a business can fund its operations. If all business partners chip in to fund the affiliate business, the financial risk will be divided.

In the beginning, the first few people you will convince to use your affiliate links are your family and friends. Your friends and family members will be the first group of people who will see the content and marketing materials you share in your social networking accounts.

With a partner, the reach of your organic marketing will significantly increase. You will be able to double the amount of people who sees your marketing materials if both partners share the content with their personal social media accounts.

5. Shiny Object Syndrome

Another reason why most affiliate marketers fail is because of what is known in the industry as the "shiny object syndrome". This phenomenon is common among entrepreneurs. The minds of entrepreneurs are so active in looking for business opportunities that it continues even when they are already working on a business. Many of the entrepreneurs who lack discipline jump from one business opportunity to another. In the middle of working on an affiliate marketing project, they decide to abandon it and start doing another type of business. This usually happens when the first idea takes too long to start showing progress.

You can avoid this common mistake by plotting the steps that you need to take to reach your goal and holding yourself accountable for reaching these goals. Consider that if you start with another project while you are in the middle of another one, you will go back to square one. Instead, you should just take note of your business ideas for you to start later on. For now, put all your focus, energy and effort on the current project you are working on. The more time and resources you put on this project, the better its chances will be of becoming successful.

6. Not delegating tasks

Affiliate marketing is a business. All businesspeople need to use the power of delegating to be successful. Creating a successful community for your affiliate marketing offers will require a lot of work. You will need to write hundreds of thousands of words of content. You will also need to create hundreds of hours' worth of video and audio content.

Creating content is more than just writing or recording. You also need to do a lot of research before writing, proofread your articles, edit your videos, create featured images for your blog posts, and create thumbnail images for YouTube.

The point is that your success depends on thousands of hours of work. To become successful, you will need help. This is where a VA can help you. VA stands for virtual assistant. To hire a real assistant, you will need to consider many factors like his or her pay, benefits, tools for working and other things. A VA on the other hand, is hired by a third-party company. You only pay the company a fraction of what you would normally pay a full time personal assistant. In turn, they will provide you with an assistant that has the skills that you need for your business.

Today's Virtual Assistants come in different forms. Some of them are jack-of-all-trades. They can do pretty much everything from writing your content to editing your YouTube videos. There are also some types of VA with specialized skills. Some can act as a personal assistant, answering emails and scheduling appointments for you so that you no longer have to deal with these kinds of tasks. Some specialize in specific industries, like real estate, accounting, finance and many more.

You can also use VAs to get some of your tasks off your plate. If you do not have the skills for editing your own videos for example, you can look for a VA with this kind of skillset. You can agree on a price and start on a per-project basis. If they deliver in terms of the quality of work and deadlines, you could hire them again for future projects. If their quality of work or work ethic is problematic, you have the choice to give them another chance or to let them go.

Finding a good employee is just as complicated online as it is offline. It may take you a few tries before you find one that works well for your business process.

7. Failing to track results

After building your affiliate marketing assets, you cannot just sit back and wait for the business to make you money. You need to continue observing the system you've developed and examine how it could be improved. Examine each step that your customers take before they end up making a purchase and find ways to improve their success rate. In some cases, you may need to improve your activities in gathering traffic. There may also be some improvements needed in converting your traffic into paying customers.

You can only learn what improvements are needed if your track the important data in your website. Luckily, you can do this free with tools like Google Analytics, Google Webmaster Tools, Twitter Analytics, Facebook Pixels and other forms of website activity tracking technology. They are easy to set up but the insights they provide can be the different between success and failure.

Chapter 8 Quiz
Please refer to Appendix H for the answers to this quiz

1. Which statement is true?

    A) You can only promote affiliate links in your website
    B) You can only promote affiliate links in your blog posts
    C) You can only promote affiliate links by spamming social media
    D) You can promote affiliate links in many places online

2. What do you call a person who trusts your vision enough to invest in your business and work with you to make it succeed?

    A) Virtual Assistant
    B) Business Partner
    C) Angel Investor
    D) Affiliate

3. What is an advantage of having a partner?

    A) Bigger operational capital
    B) Easier working process
    C) Larger affiliate sales numbers
    D) Faster spread of content in search engines

4. How do you track your sales numbers?

    A) Through the affiliate dashboard stats area
    B) Through the commission you receive
    C) Through Google Analytics
    D) Through Social Media Insights

5. What do people hate when they are looking for good content about a product?

    A) Engaging videos
    B) Images of the product in use
    C) Exaggerated claims
    D) Formal grammar

6. What is an example of an exaggerated claim?

    A) This laptop has 4GB of RAM
    E) This phone can be submerged until six inches of water

F) The casing is made from aluminum

G) This chair is the best computer chair I've ever seen in my entire life

7. How does the "Shiny Object Syndrome" affect your success?

A) It allows you to accomplish more tasks in lesser time

B) It doubles you productivity at night

C) It prevents you from finishing projects

D) It prevents you from selling affiliate products

8. What do you call workers who can do specific tasks for you over the internet?

A) Virtual assistants

B) Drones

C) Crowdsourcing

D) Ghostwriters

9. Which of the following statements is true?

A) Virtual assistants are good only for menial tasks

B) Virtual assistants will steal your ideas

C) Some virtual assistants have specialized skills

D) Virtual assistants are too expensive for the affiliate marketing business

10. Which of the following statements is true?

A) You can succeed only by delegating all your tasks to virtual assistants

B) You can succeed by doing everything things on your own

C) You can start delegating tasks to lessen the workload on yourself

D) Virtual assistants cannot be trusted

Inspiration #9

"Don't be afraid to give up the good to go for the great."
John D. Rockefeller

Chapter 9

Choosing the Right Niche

Choosing the right niche is just as important as choosing the right affiliate program to join. Many beginners start out just making affiliate marketing websites for the first topic that enters their minds. Three months into the project, they are no longer motivated to work on the topic. This is one of the primary reasons why beginner affiliate marketers quit on their project. In this section, we will discuss how you can choose the best niche for you:

Make a list of your hobbies, interests and passions

First, you will need to make a list of the hobbies, interests and passions you have in life. Consider the things that you spend the most of your time in. You could also include a topic about your occupation if you enjoy talking about it. Also, think about the topics that you would like to learn. Choose at least 15 topics and list them down.

Arrange the topics you've chosen according to how much you enjoy talking about them

Next, you should arrange the topics based on how much you enjoy it. Right off the bat, you will notice that there are some topics that you enjoy more than others. Look into these topics first when you are deciding on an affiliate marketing niche.

Survey other people's interest about the subject

Starting with the first topic on your list, you should start researching the interest of other people in the topic. You want to start working on a topic that people are interested in. You can start by surveying the content in your big traffic sources (Google Search, Facebook, Twitter, and Instagram). You could do a quick Google search about the topic and take note of the content that comes out. You could also look into the content marketing accounts in social networks that deal with this type of content. You can guess the popularity of a topic based on the number of engagement they get in social media.

Survey the competition

If you are satisfied with the amount of interest that that a topic gets, you should check the competition in the market about it next. You probably already encountered some of your content marketing competition when you were doing the previous step. Any website that is doing some sort of content marketing is one of your competition because they are trying to take your target audience's attention away. The more competition you have, the harder it will be for you to stand out in the content market place.

Ideally, you should pick a topic with the least amount of competition. However, at times, you can succeed in a high-competition niche by narrowing your content's focus only on the more profitable topics. With the topic recreational running for example, you could choose to focus only on the topic of running gear. You could share content about the latest and best running shoes, clothing and gadgets in the market.

Find the most commonly searched problems about this niche

Now that you have a niche in mind, start planning the types of content that you will create. You should start writing about the content before you even set up your affiliate marketing website. This way, you will be able to start promoting the moment the website is live.

To find topics to talk about, you should start with the problems that people interested in the niche face. If you are just learning about the topic yourself, you should look into the problems that beginners tend to run into. This way, you will also be writing with a beginner's point of view.

Find affiliate products that can solve the problems in these niches

After choosing the niche based on its popularity and the amount of competition in the market, you should look into the available affiliate products you can sell in that niche. You could start by looking for products that will solve the problems established in the previous step.

The easiest way to start is to look for products and brands in Amazon. Amazon sells pretty much everything. If you cannot find the product that you would like to promote in other companies, there is a good chance that it will be available in Amazon.

Amazon though has a low commission rate. To get better commission rates, you should check if the product you want to promote can be found in other affiliate networks discussed previously.

Chapter 9 Quiz
Please refer to Appendix H for the answers to this quiz

1. What do you call a small segment of a larger market where certain products can focus their marketing efforts?

   A) Finance market
   B) Business to Business Market
   C) Niche Market
   D) Open Market

2. How does focusing on a niche market help your website?

   A) It attracts a group of people with specialized needs
   B) It allows the website to attract a bigger number of visitors
   C) It gives the websites opportunities for special promotions
   D) It increases the number of possible content

3. How do you start finding the right niche for you?

   A) Ask the people around me for the best niches
   B) Explore my own hobbies and interests
   C) Look for products online
   D) Build the website and see which content ranks well

4. How do you check if other people are interested about the niche topic?

   A) Visit popular news websites regularly
   B) Ask your friends and family if they will be interested about it
   C) Check related content in social media and the amount of engagement they get
   D) Do an initial ad campaign about the topic

5. Which topic should you take?

   A) Topic with the most competition
   B) Topic with no competition
   C) Topic that has more products associated with it
   D) Topics that has one expensive product associated with it

6. How do you differentiate your website from the strong competitors in the niche market?

   A) Copy the content of the competitors
   B) Pick a specialized niche topic that few people have talked about

C) Post 5 or more contents every day

D) Use a catchy domain name

7. How do you look for content on your chosen niche topic?

A) Make things up

B) Research on the common problems that people encounter when researching about the topic

C) Research on the ways on how you can promote products to visitors

D) Buy products in your niche and review them

8. If you are writing how-to contents about the niche topic, who are likely to come to your website?

A) Random people

B) Experts in the topic

C) Beginners in the topic

D) People who need to solve the how-to problem

9. If you are writing news content about the niche topic where will your content be most effective?

A) Search engines

B) Social Media

C) Forums

D) Question and Answer websites

10. If you've chosen the basketball sneakers niche, which type of content should you create and share?

A) Articles about the latest sneakers in the market

B) Articles about girlfriend of basketball stars

C) Videos about basketball highlights

D) Videos about rumors and gossips in basketball

Inspiration #10

"Successful people do what unsuccessful people are not willing to do. Don't wish it were easier; wish you were better."

Jim Rohn

Chapter 10

Building your Email List

Many of the people who go to your website will not necessarily click on the affiliate link. Most of them will just leave without taking any action that helps your business. You can use an email marketing campaign to keep a percentage of these people coming back to your website. Email marketing is effective because it makes you part of one of the most common habits among professionals, checking emails.

People treat emails with a higher level of priority compared to other forms of communication because it is usually used for work. Checking one's emails is one of the first things that most people do when they get to work. By setting up an affiliate marketing campaign, you will be able to put your affiliate marketing business in the screens of people who do have the power and the willingness to buy the products you promote.

To implement an effective email marketing campaign, you will need to learn the steps on how to make people sign up and how to use email newsletters to keep them coming back to your website. The basic steps of an affiliate marketing campaign come in three basic steps:

❖ Capturing emails
❖ Automated response
❖ Sending out newsletters and email-exclusive promotions

Experts say that it takes at least seven interactions with your brand before the average new customer decides to buy. If you want new visitors to come to your shop and buy using your affiliate links, you will need to make them keep coming back to your website, constantly. An email campaign is an effective way to do this. First though, you will need to convince your visitors to give up their email addresses.

You can do this through your content marketing campaign. In your website, you could set up an email capturing tool that appears together with the content. The placement of these email capturing forms is important. Here are the places where you should be placing them:

Before your content

An email form before the content will ensure that the visitors see it. In this position, more people will see it and a higher number of visitors may sign up. Make sure though that it occupies only a small part of the screen and it can be dismissed.

In-content

Most online readers have developed a habit to skip everything above the fold and go straight to the content. Their eyes go from the title of the article straight to the first paragraph. For visitors with this kind of habit, you can put your email capturing tool inside the article. This strategy works because you can use the text in the content or the other types of media to bring attention to the email subscription form.

In pop-ups

Pop ups can be good or bad depending on how you use it. If you use it to promote unwanted ads, then people will hate your website. In the case of email subscription popups on the other hand, you are actually offering something that people may like.

The best part about popups is that you can choose an action that will trigger it. For instance, some popups are triggered after you have spent a considerable amount of time in the website. Some of them are also triggered by activities like clicks or pressing the close button to leave the page. With these triggers, you can capture the emails of visitors based on their intended activity in the website. You can have it triggered for example by a call-to-action button. Or, you can also capture it when the person is about to leave.

In the Sidebar

In the past, bloggers and content marketers mostly put their email subscription forms in the sidebar. This makes the form easily visible, especially if it is placed above the fold. Unfortunately, because of the use of the sidebar for placing ads, internet users have generally developed the habit of avoiding looking at the sidebars. Because of this, the effectiveness of forms placed in this section has decreases.

The increase in the use of mobile devices to view websites has also made sidebars less effective. In a mobile-responsive theme, the sidebars are placed under the content. This means that your forms at the sidebar will only be viewed after the visitor read the content. Unfortunately, between 40-60% of readers never get to the bottom of articles. If you post mostly long articles, expect that the sidebar forms will be ignored. If you post short posts on the other hand, a large part of your traffic may reach the bottom of your content and more people will see your forms.

AMP Pages and Facebook Instant Articles

Facebook and Google are both promoting the use of stripped down pages for mobile devices to increase the speed of webpage loading. Google calls this type of webpage AMP or accelerated mobile pages. Facebook has its own version of this and they call it Facebook Instant Articles.

Both of these traffic sources have guidelines on how to create these types of pages. For Google, you only need to create a special part of your website dedicated to AMP. This type of page is stripped down its usual features. Any extra code is removed and only the essentials are left.

For Facebook Instant Articles, you will need to create alternate versions of your content inside of Facebook. The Instant Articles will be hosted by Facebook themselves and you will need to pass an application process to be able to use this feature.

These types of pages are effective in collecting emails because they are fast loading and they tend to have higher capturing rates compared to the average webpage. The lack of distractions in the AMP and the Facebook Instant Articles makes it easier for people to see the email form you set up. In the case of Facebook instant articles, the email address of the Facebook user is already typed in the form. A user only needs to click the subscribe button to sign up to your email newsletter.

Other social networks

You can also get more email newsletters from the other social media assets you have. If you have an Instagram page for instance, make use of it by mentioning your email newsletters in your post descriptions. You could then add the link to your email subscription form in the bio. This is a much better approach than just to drive Instagram users to your latest content. It will consistently create a call to action that can lead to returning visitors.

Aside from Instagram, you could also mention your email newsletters in your personal and business twitter page. Together with your regular marketing posts, you could include a call-to-action link leading to your subscription form pages. It will be challenging for you to craft a good copy in twitter because of the limit in the number of characters that you can use. You can use other types of media though, like images and videos, to capture the attention of your audience better.

Above, we talked about Facebook Instant Articles. This is not the only way though to collect emails from Facebook. You can also put your email subscription link in the description of your Facebook content. While Instant Articles can also be effective in spreading the news about your website, contents like videos and viral images will have an even greater reach to your audiences in Facebook.

To start, you should pick one piece of content that you will use as your carrier. Ideally, you should choose the type of content that has no other call-to-action feature. For example, you can use a how-to video in your niche. You could also use an image that you think your target market can relate to. If you are satisfied with the content, you could then post it in your Facebook page.

In the description section of your content, you could then add a paragraph for promoting your email subscription form. In this section you could state some of the benefits that they can get for signing up. Together with the text marketing copy, you can then add a link to your sign up form.

Creating a Lead Capture/Squeeze page

A lead capture page is a type of landing page designed to capture opt-in email addresses from potential subscribers. The goal of a squeeze page is to convince, cajole, or otherwise "squeeze" a visitor into providing one of their most sought-after and coveted pieces of personal data: the email address. An example squeeze page is shown below:

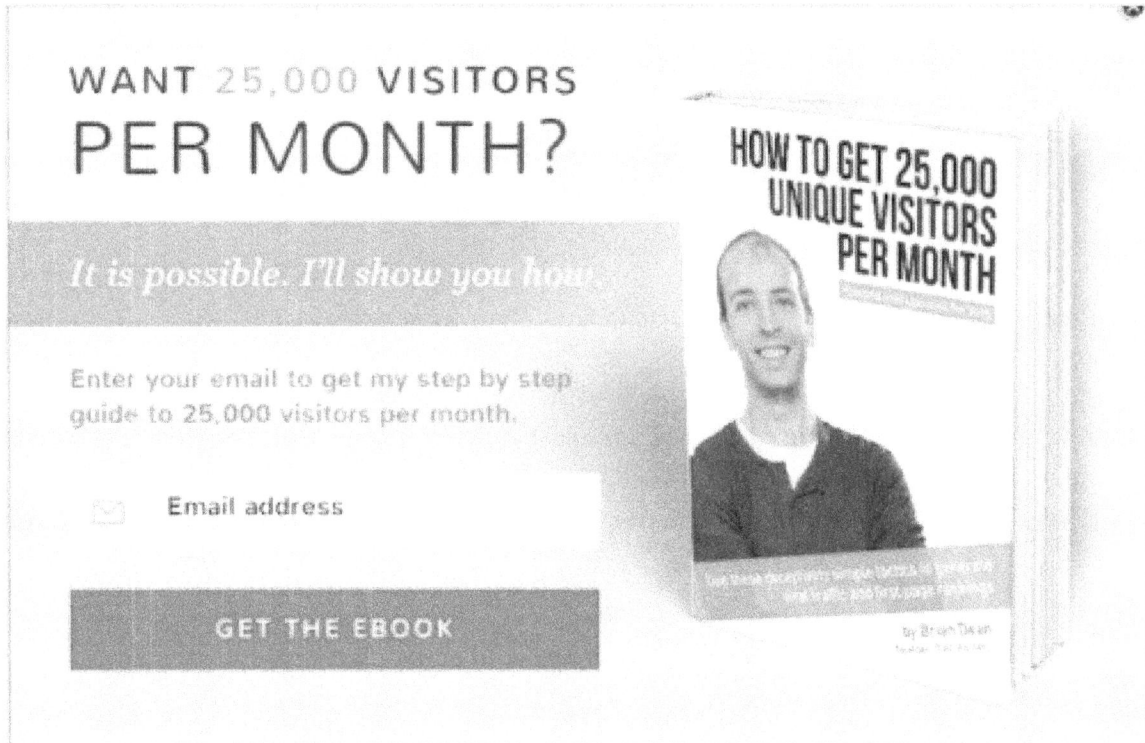

To be successful collecting leads, your capture pages need to have the right balance of "ask" and "reward." The "ask" are the form fields you use, and the "reward" is the offer you're promoting.

A lead capture page that asks visitors for irrelevant information to the offer is abandoned because a poorly-optimized lead capture form is one of the leading causes of landing page friction. Ideally, your form should not ask for more than basic contact information on the user's first interaction with your company.

A number of companies provide softwares that help you design these capture pages. One of the good ones out there is clickfunnels. Below are the reasons why:

➢ Clickfunnels provides you with a LOT of pre-built funnel templates. For those who have never designed a funnel before this will be perfect for you!
➢ Great visual drag and drop editor which is very beginner friendly
➢ Huge selection of page elements (name field, telephone number, countdown timer etc.)
➢ The ability to share your funnels with your friends and clients!
➢ Amazing onboarding process - Wrapping your head around all that ClickFunnels can do may seem daunting at first. But this is helped by a fun on-boarding process. When you first sign up, you're presented with the 7-day challenge. It consists of 4 different games with each one having a number of steps to complete. Every step features a task and a short video clip of Russell explaining what you need to do to finish it.
➢ If you're interested in getting a 14 days free trial, go to the clickfunnels website or my website at www.MichaelEzeanaka.com (disclaimer – I am an affiliate)

Limit the number of times you ask for visitors' emails

People do not like it if you keep pestering them with intrusive call-to-action features. You do not want people to leave because your marketing campaign is too aggressive. With this in mind, you should limit your popups to just one per session. You can even program popup plugins in WordPress to stop showing to repeat visitors. This will ensure that your visitors will not get the wrong impression from your aggressive ways of capturing emails.

Ask for emails in a natural way

The language you use when asking for email addresses affects the effectiveness of your tools. Ideally, you should talk in the language of your average visitor. If you are talking to professionals for instance, you can use formal English to talk to them so that they are more likely to engage. If you are talking to young adults for instance, try to use modern colloquialism that young adults use. Your familiarity of your target audience plays a big role in your ability to create your call-to-action statements.

State your email campaign's unique value proposition in your email subscription forms

People will not just automatically sign up to your email newsletter service just because you have your forms set up. You still need to convince them to sign up by promising them the right things. We call this part your unique value proposition. This is a paragraph or a statement that comes with you subscription form where you state the benefits of signing up. You could tell them what they will get for signing up to your website.

Think of different ways for you to get the attention of your viewers towards your signup forms. Some affiliate marketers for instance, give out free digital products like a free eBook or a free trial to a service, to encourage people to sign up to the email campaign. You can also do the same. One way to do this is to create an awesome eBook that fits the interest of your niche market. You could then sell the eBook to Amazon and other eBook selling platforms. Doing this will allow you to establish the value of your books. After setting it up in these websites, offer a free version of your book in your website, telling them that they will be able to read the book for free if they sign up to your email service.

In the process, you could also explain the other things that they can get for signing up to your email newsletters. You could state what types of content you send out and how often you send them out. For instance, you could tell them that you have a video tutorial series that are available only to email newsletter subscribers.

Creating many types of lists

As your website grows, you will eventually find that you have multiple categories of content. This can lead to attracting audience that has different interests and goals for coming to your website. If you are attracting a heterogeneous traffic, you may need to create multiple types of email lists, categorized according to the interests and goals of your market. If the person first arrived in an article about planting green leafy vegetables for instance, you could have him sign up in a newsletter that promises content about planting green leafy vegetables. You also notice that great deal of your visitors is attracted towards your articles and videos about composting. You can create a different type of list exclusively for these people.

It goes without saying that you will need to craft very different autoresponder messages for these two lists. The welcome message and future messages should be related to the interests of your subscriber. You could also create a different list based on the buying stage of the subscriber. You could create an email list for beginners for instance. You could create another one for those who are interested in advanced level contents. Beginners for a topic will need a different set of content and affiliate offers compared to those who are already in the advanced or expert levels.

You could then create a sales funnel. In a sales funnel, you try to convert passive readers of your email newsletters into buyers of your offers. You can do this by adjusting the content that you send to your subscribers, from entertaining and informational to contents that suggest buying products and services.

Engaging with the customer

You should capitalize on the hype that the visitors get when they sign up with your email campaign. The energy and enthusiasm of subscribers are highest at this point. When they sign up, they are eager to see what types of content you have to offer in your email marketing campaign.

Creating your autoresponders

The signup process for email newsletters is pretty straightforward. After signing up with your email subscription form, your subscribers will expect a welcome email. You can set this up with your autoresponder service.

Create your content with your chosen email marketing management service. The email should read in a warm manner, making your new subscribers feel welcome. If you made any promises in the sign up process, you can start fulfilling them in the welcome email. If you promised a free eBook for instance, you should have the link to your eBook in the welcome email of your newsletter.

In addition to the welcome email, you should create more content related to your unique value proposition in the email subscription process. If you promised unique types of content in your email, you could craft them ahead of time and have them sent out daily through your autoresponders. Let's say that your website is about home keeping. You could begin by creating list article where in you talk about 5 ways to keep the home organized. Instead of showing the entire article to your audience however, you could have the content drip in the email newsletter auto responder. You could then have them scheduled to be sent out twice a week so that people will anticipate them.

Make sure that the content in your welcome emails and in the succeeding auto-response to be substantial so that people will find them valuable. If your email subscribers do not view these emailed content valuable, they may end up ignoring your emails or they may choose to unsubscribe.

To automate the process of sending out these autoresponders, you could use email campaign management services like Aweber. With this tool, you can create prepared emails with the names of the future subscriber in the content. You can also set up the emails to send every week. As at the time of writing, they do an initial 30-day free trial. Alternatively, feel free to check it out at my website (disclaimer – I am an affiliate).

Choose your email marketing approach

There is more than one way to craft your autoresponders and email newsletters. In this section, we will discuss the different approaches and email layouts you can use to create your emails.

The personal approach

If you website is heavily reliant on your personality, you may need to use the personal approach in creating your emails. With this method, you are communicating towards your subscribers as if you are writing a letter to them. The goal of any content you add is to create a personal relationship with the subscriber.

This method requires that you show your face throughout the email marketing process. It begins with the sign up process. In your sign up form, you could enhance the effectiveness of your opt-in tools by putting your own smiling face beside it. People love to join email marketing campaigns wherein they know who is behind it. By putting your own image with the marketing materials, you are establishing the trust between you and the subscriber. Remember that you are asking them to give up their email address at this point. For most people, giving up an email address is a sign that they are giving you're their trust. The best part about this is that you will significantly increase the success rate of your opt-in tools. People are more likely to signup if they see a familiar face.

The personal touch continues with the rest of the content that you send to the subscriber's emails. It begins with the welcome email. Together with your picture, you could also write a letter that sounds welcoming and personal. The idea is to thank your news subscribers by personally welcoming them into the program.

To continue this approach, you should aim to write personalized letters to your subscribers as a way to introduce your email content. The more interactions you have with these people, the better your relationship with them will be. With this kind of relationship in place, they are more likely to follow your suggestions and your recommendations. This will lead to higher sales numbers.

The brand approach

If you do not like putting your face in all your marketing tools, you may also choose to use the brand approach. In this approach, your aim is to have your subscribers trust your website, rather than your real persona. While many big businesses use this approach, it may take time for you to develop a brand name and to have people trust that brand.

With this approach however, you will be able to distance yourself from the business. With the personal approach, you need to be present to continue creating email content for your subscribers. They expect personal treatment from you.

With the brand approach on the other hand, the trust is with the brand that you have developed. Because of this, it will be easier for you to delegate task to the people around you. You can send out an email to your list with a less personal note and no one will notice because they trust the brand rather than your persona.

To start with this approach, you need to create uniform way of presenting your brand. To start with, you should decide on a brand name, a tag line and a logo. The brand name will be the name that your visitors will use when talking about your website. The tagline is a short phrase that tells new audiences about what your brand is about. The brand name and tagline should be easy to understand and say. They should roll off the tongue easily. You will also need to design a logo that represents what you stand for. Make your logo characteristics match the overall theme of your brand. If your website is about gardening for instance, your logo could be green and it could have images related to gardening. You can have such a logo professionally created for $5 in Fiverr.com.

To develop your website's brand, you need to show people that your website is a reliable source of information. To do this, you need to make sure that the website is already complete by the time you launch it. There should be no lacking aspect of your website. This will show that the website is backed by competent professionals. Next, you will need to add content to your website in a consistent manner. The content in both your website and your social media marketing assets should be professionally done. Ideally, they should be unique and not copied from other website.

Now that you have established that you run a professional website, the next step is to make this reflect in your email marketing campaign. While people using the personal approach can get away with sloppy newsletters, brands cannot. It is easy to forgive a person for common mistakes but it is significantly harder to forgive brands.

Inspiration #11

"Don't let the fear of losing be greater than the excitement of winning."

Robert Kiyosaki

Chapter 10 Quiz
Please refer to Appendix I for the answers to this quiz

1. What is the primary purpose of an email marketing campaign?

    A) Increase affiliate sales
    B) Keep people coming back to your website
    C) To send people unwanted messages
    D) To reach strangers who have never been to your website before

2. What do you call the emails that are automatically sent after a person signs up?

    A) Autosender
    B) Autorepeater
    C) Autoresponder
    D) Autoblogger

3. What is an example of an email campaign management service?

    A) GoDaddy
    B) Aweber
    C) Facebook Pixels
    D) Google AdWords

4. What do you call the faster, stripped down version of webpages used by Google for displaying content in mobile devices

    A) AMP
    B) CBS
    C) BBD
    D) Instant Articles

5. How do you share your email subscription form in Instagram?

    A) Put a link of it in your bio and mention the link in your posts
    B) Put a link in your bio and the description of your posts
    C) Use private messaging to reach random people
    D) Comment the link in the images and videos of celebrities

6. In which placement position is an email form most likely to be engaged with?

A) In the sidebar

B) In-content

C) In the footer

D) In a new window pop-up

7. This is the part of the email subscription call-to-action that states the offer that only you can give the audience. You offer this feature to them in exchange for giving up their email addresses in the form…

    A) Free products

    B) Instant promotion

    C) Email newsletters

    D) Unique value proposition

8. Which practice should you avoid when showing your email subscription form?

    A) Put the form in the body of the article

    B) Show the form in 3 pop-ups for each visitor

    C) Put the form in your social media accounts

    D) Talk about the unique value proposition in the sign up

9. What is a good example of a freebie that you can give people to encourage them to sign up?

    A) Free eBook

    B) Membership to an exclusive websites

    C) Free coffee beans

    D) Discount with one of your promoted affiliate programs

10. What are the two approaches for talking with your audience through email?

    A) Brand and Personal approaches

    B) Business and Social approaches

    C) Single and Married approaches

    D) High-ticket and low-ticket approaches

Chapter 11

Affiliate Marketing Strategies

An effective affiliate marketing strategy should be efficient. One way to ensure this is by keeping the number of clicks between the traffic source and the affiliate marketing landing page as few as possible. The fewer clicks it requires to reach the affiliate marketing website, the higher your conversion rate will be.

If you post your affiliate link directly to Facebook for example, there will be only one click between the source and the affiliate landing page. This is the shortest route between the traffic source (Facebook) and the landing page.

The model looks something like this:

Facebook > Affiliate Marketing Landing Page

In most cases however, this marketing model is not effective because most people are likely to avoid your content if it only contains an affiliate link. It may work to some degree in the beginning. Eventually though, your success rate will go down. Your audience will eventually catch on with what you are trying to do and they may avoid your post.

In addition, convincing people to move from a traffic source to the affiliate marketing landing page can be difficult. Most people do not want to move away from their social networks or their preferred websites. People only willingly click away from these websites or apps if they are motivated to do so. Most people would only move away from their Facebook or Twitter apps if there is an article they want to read or a video they want to watch.

The most successful content marketers use a different approach. They first send their traffic to their website content, where they can convince them to buy the product. They use the content marketing strategies, similar to the ones discussed in this book, to drive traffic from the traffic source to their websites. The model looks like this:

Facebook (Sample Traffic Source) > Website Content > Affiliate Marketing Landing Page

In this model, the process is still somewhat efficient because there are only two clicks between the traffic source and the affiliate marketing landing page. With this model, it will be easier for you to lure your target audience from the traffic source with the use of the right types of contents.

Track the movement of your users

When you are successfully sending traffic to your website through the various traffic sources, you need to set up your analytic tools to track how people move in your website. In the beginning, a big portion of your traffic will bounce. Bouncing refers to the act of leaving a website after viewing just one page. People usually bounce when the content in the website did not pique their interest. This is common with news websites where the average bounce rate is just above 80%. This means that 80% of the traffic leaves the website after reading just one news story.

As an affiliate marketer, you want your viewers to keep reading your content, transferring from one page to another. If this happens, it means that your contents are effective in keeping the attention of your website users. With this method, you will be able to track the movements of the users and identify the types of content that they are likely to click on.

You could also track the total number of clicks that your affiliate links get. The most accurate number will be posted in the statistics portion of your affiliate marketing account. In affiliate programs like Amazon Affiliates and ClickBank, these clicks are shown directly in your account dashboard. You can get the total success rate of your website in sending people to the affiliate landing pages by dividing the total number of clicks on your affiliate links by the total number of unique visitors to your website in a given period. You could then multiply the quotient by 100% to get the percentage value.

Let's say that you want to get your website's success rate for an entire week. You should take the total number of clicks on your affiliate links (found in your affiliate account) and the total number of unique visitors for the week (found in your website analytics) for the said period. You could then use this formula to get the effectiveness of your website in converting users:

Success rate = (number of clicks/total number of unique visitors) * 100%

Let' say that for that week 2,500 unique visitors went to your website. Of that number, 50 people clicked on your affiliate links. Using the formula above, we will get a success rate of 2%. With the success rate, you will be able to predict how well your website performs in sending people to an affiliate landing page in the future.

Judge each affiliate program based on their landing pages

The success rate metric alone however, is not enough to predict how much you will earn in the future. To get this prediction, you will need to get the average conversion rate of the landing page. The advertisers' landing pages are supposed to be designed to increase conversion. A 2-4% conversion rate is normal for a non-optimized affiliate landing page. These numbers can significantly increase to 10% and up if the advertisers test different pages and stick to the page layouts and designs that lead to the most conversions.

Online advertising professionals put a lot of time, working on increasing the conversion rates of their landing pages. However, some landing pages just work better than others. If all other factors are equal, you will earn more if you promote an affiliate program with an excellent landing page. Because of this, you want to stick only with advertisers whose landing page performs well. Unfortunately, you can only check how well a landing page performs by sending leads to it and measuring the results.

The conversion rate of a landing page is usually shown in the analytics section of your affiliate marketing account. If this is not the case however, you could calculate this yourself. To do this, you first need to find the total number of leads (unique visitors) you sent to a particular landing page. This should be reflected in the number of clicks that a particular affiliate link gets. You will also need the total number of sales generated for that particular link. You can usually get this number in the sales report section of your affiliate account.

You can then divide the number of sales by the number of leads you sent and multiple the result by 100%. A higher percentage means that the landing page is effective in converting leads into customers. Sometimes, different websites will have completely different conversion rates even if they are sending traffic to the same landing page. This happens because many factors affect the success of a landing page. We will discuss them in the following section. You can check these factors whenever you are inspecting a new landing page of an advertiser

Factors that affect landing page conversion rate:

The design and layout of the page

You can choose advertisers based on the design and layout of their landing page. If a landing page has no published conversion rate, you may need to base your decision to use it based on these two superficial factors.

Ideally, the design should focus on the purchasing features of the page. The landing page's sole purpose is to convince the people viewing it to make a purchase. If the page has too many distractions or if the purchase buttons are too small to be seen, this may lead to a low conversion rate.

An effective way of checking the design and layout of an affiliate landing page is by using the help of your loved ones. Before you use a landing page, let the people you know check it out first. You could have a questionnaire ready when they check these landing pages. You will need to ask them the following questions:

1. From a scale of 1-10, how likely are you to buy from this page?
2. Do you see a purchase button or link immediately?
3. How do you find the design?
   - Distracting or too cluttered
   - Helpful for buyers
   - Unattractive or outdated
   - Informative or educational
4. If you like the product being promoted, are you going from this page or are you going to find another source of the same product? Why?

By letting the people you know check the landing page and answer the questions above, you will be able to get an idea of how an average person with no marketing background views the page. You will be able to get multiple opinions on the quality of the page. If you just base your judgment on your own opinion, you may have personal biases that may prevent you from choosing the best landing page. Knowing what other people think about the page will help make your decision of choosing a landing page objective.

The quality of traffic that you send to it

At times, an affiliate marketer may get a lower conversion rate than the published rate of a landing page. The affiliate network metrics for example, may say that a landing page gets 7% conversion rate but it only converted 3% of the traffic you sent to it. This may happen when the quality of the traffic you send to the landing page is not at par with the industry standards.

Here are the qualities of the visitors that you should send to your affiliate marketing landing pages:

A. They should have a buying intent

Landing pages work best if you send people to it who are already in the verge of buying the product. This factor is most important to people who are buying something pricey. Low-ticket items are open to impulse buys. A person with no buying intent may buy a $5 shirt from an online retailer without thinking too much about it. Everything changes when more money is on the line. Consider your own personal process when buying something expensive. Do you research first or do you buy impulsively?

Before an average person buys a new laptop for example, they first look around for the newest models from different brands. They then, collect information on the features that are important for them. A person on a budget for example, may take note of the prices of the different models. A computer gaming enthusiast on the other hand, may not be as interested in the prices as he or she is in the performance specs of the laptop. Only after people have collected enough information are they likely to make a buying decision.

You can make sure that the people you refer to your affiliate links have buying intentions by adjusting the types of content in your website. If you already have a website with a lot of articles and other contents, check each of them. Assess your website contents and check whether they are important in the beginning, middle or end of the buying process. Plot the normal buying process for the products you promote. Then, you should create content that will capture more people who are towards the end of the process.

Let's say you are promoting action cameras in your website. You use a GoPro to record your activities like playing with your dog, playing sports, going on vacations, etc. With the content you share in social media, you are able to attract a lot of users from social networks.

The problem with this method of gaining traffic is that the people you attract do not necessarily have buying intentions. They are only there to view the photos and videos you took with your GoPro. Because they do not have a buying intent, they are less likely to click on your affiliate links. To convert these people from being passive audiences into buyers, you will need to create multiple contents (articles and videos) where you can naturally promote the action camera. For example, you can film your trip to a local vacation spot and make a how-to article and video about how to get there and what to do when you are there. In the process, you can write that their experience will be greatly enhanced if they bring an action camera with them. You could then include an affiliate link in your article. In the video you create, you can talk about the same thing and mention that you have link in the description of the video for the item you are recommending.

Aside from these types of contents, you can also create series of contents that are designed to highlight the product you are promoting. For example, you can write an article of record a vlog talking about your own buying decision when you bought the action camera. You can also make a comparison article or video, comparing the product you are promoting with competing brands. Lastly, you can talk about the prices of the product from different sources and the discount coupons they can use to save money when purchasing.

As a recap, here are the types of contents that you should create:

1. Articles and videos to a local tourist spot where you use the action camera
   - Target Audience: Beginners and Social Media Users
2. Article and video about your personal buying decision
   - Target Audience: Beginners and Social Media Users
3. Comparison article and video against competing brands
   - Target Audience: People with buying intent, Google Searchers
4. Article and video talking about the price and the best sources of the product
   - Target Audience: People with buying intent, Google Searchers

These are only some ideas on the types of content you can create for this particular product. You can create all these articles and videos in a matter of weeks. You should also consider not stopping with these four contents. You can create more articles and videos about going to the different tourist attractions in your area. Aside from the action camera itself, you can also make product reviews about its different accessories. Just keep creating content about it and how to use it and people will eventually buy it.

B. They should be capable of buying the product

There is no use promoting your website in places where the majority of people are not capable of buying your product. If you are promoting products from Amazon.com for example, you should make sure that you are promoting to people from the US. Make sure that the tips and recommendations you post on your articles and videos are significant to US consumers. The same goes for the coupons and other promotions you offer.

Aside from ensuring that you are promoting to people from the right location, you should also make sure that the people you are promoting to have the necessary tools for purchasing. This means that they should have access to a credit card or any other method of payment allowed by the retailer you are promoting.

Promoting affiliate products towards children for example, is not just against that law but also ineffective. Children do not have the financial freedom to purchase the product themselves.

C. Shopping seasons and the level of competition in the market

The conversion rate of a landing page will also be affected by the season. A landing page that has a high conversion rate in regular days may experience a dip in its effectiveness during the holidays when there are many other competing offers in the market. In the US for example, the time around thanksgiving and Christmas is usually considered shopping season. People love the promotions in these days. If the products in the landing page that you are using are still offered at their regular prices in these times of the year, your visitors may choose to buy the competing brands or from others sources of the item where there are discounts.

As a response, you should always keep track of the different competing offers in the market. Check the different source for the products that you are offering. If you see that the other sources of the products are offering discounts, you can talk to your affiliate marketing manager about it.

Chapter 11 Quiz
Please refer to Appendix J for the answers to this quiz

1. How do you keep your affiliate marketing strategy efficient?

    A) Keeping ads expenses low
    B) Using a cheap hosting package
    C) Keeping the number of clicks low between the traffic source and landing page
    D) Using hosted blog platforms like blogger

2. Why is posting affiliate links directly in public ineffective?

    A) It may be copied by other people
    B) People will go directly to the website without going through the link
    C) People will avoid clicking on it, thinking it's spam
    D) It is against the rules

3. What motivational trick can we use to make people click on shared content?

    A) Use great headlines and featured image
    B) Promise free gifts
    C) Offer them money for clicking
    D) Use bright colors in the post

4. What do we call the event wherein the person leaves the website after viewing just one page?

    A) Trounce
    B) Bounce
    C) Once
    D) Exit

5. How do you make an intelligent guess if an affiliate link has a high conversion rate before even making it live?

    A) Examine the landing page
    B) Buy the affiliate product yourself
    C) Ask your friends to clock on it
    D) Test it with children

6. What two factors affect the quality of the visitors you send to a landing page?

    A) Intent and capacity to buy
    B) Credit card brand and location of visitor

C) Country of origin of the product and the visitor

D) Religious and political orientation of the visitor

7. How to you improve click-through rates in your landing pages?

    A) Gather the right type of traffic
    B) Build more websites
    C) Post more often in social media
    D) Buy ad placements in popular websites

8. Which type of visitor has the highest intention of making a purchase?

    A) Search engine users who arrived with a product related key phrase
    E) Facebook users who clicked on your content
    F) Instagram users who clicked the link in your bio
    G) A user that came to check images

9. How does the shopping season affect the performance of landing pages?

    A) People don't buy online during holidays
    B) Bargain hunters spam landing pages to make them unusable
    C) People like to shop during this time of the year therefore, increasing the price
    D) The level of competition increases during this season, making regular offers obsolete

10. What should you do to have a competitive landing page during high volume traffic seasons?

    A) Find landing pages for competitive offers and promotions
    B) Stop affiliate marketing during the holidays
    C) Use more ads during this time of the year
    D) Keep expectations low during this time

Inspiration #12

"The way to get started is to quit talking and begin doing."

Walt Disney

Chapter 12

Tips to Become a Successful Affiliate Marketer

Success in affiliate marketing can mean earning millions of dollars every month. The very best players in the market achieve this level of earnings on a regular basis. How do you reach this level of success? Check out these tips to start:

Sell things and services that you are knowledgeable about

It is easier to become an effective affiliate marketer if you know what you are talking about. If you create a website about a niche topic, experts in the industry will eventually check your websites and view your content. The experts in the industry will know if you are only posing as an expert. If an expert in the niche exposes you, you may end up losing credibility with your audience.

As we've discussed earlier in the book, it is easier to have people obey your suggestions if they see that you are an expert in the topic. Because of this, it is ideal if you start your affiliate marketing career in a niche topic that you are an expert on.

In the beginning, focus on providing good quality content and getting traffic. Many aspiring affiliate marketers focus too much on earning their first buck. If you have this mindset from the beginning, you will be disappointed when the income is slow as you are just starting out. Instead of focusing on the income, shift your focus on the process of creating high quality content first. After you've created your first few articles and videos, turn your attention to getting people to see them. This book provides you with the tools on how you can do this part of the process. All you need to do is avoid worrying about the first few bucks and shift your focus on catering to the needs of your audience.

Keep your online assets active

Aside from creating content and driving traffic to them, you should create a system for keeping your online assets active. You will need to work hard and work smart to achieve this. In the beginning, you will not have a lot of funds to work with. You will be using your personal funds to pay for the business. Because of this, you will need to do much of the work yourself in keeping your website and your other social media assets active.
As you start to earn money, you can reinvest part of it back to the business. Instead of spending all of it, you could use part of the income to hire a VA, as suggested in earlier chapters. Hire them to do simple projects like creating a series of related articles or for managing your social network posting schedule.

Hiring a VA is worth the money if he or she can take tasks that you hate doing. If you do not like communicating with other website owners and bloggers for guest posting, you could have a VA do the email tasks for you. All you have to do is to instruct him or her on what to do, state the steps for his or her work process and supervise everything he or she does every day. By letting your VA do some of the work, you will be able to shift your focus to getting more traffic and continuing to grow your business with high quality content.

Don't stop with one website

There is a limit to the potential of a niche topic. Let's say that your website is about scuba diving and your content is focused on diving related articles and videos. In the process, you use your content to promote scuba diving related gear and equipment. Even if you do get the top spot in Google and your social media pages and accounts become super popular, your success will be limited by the number of people who are interested in scuba diving. If something happens that makes people want to avoid scuba diving (like news about scuba diving accidents), your business may suffer.

To prevent these types of events from damaging your business, you should diversify and explore other niches when you are contented with your first website. This way, you will be able to earn from other niche markets.

You will need to make sure that your first website is earning and self-sustaining before you commit to working on another one. This way, you can leave the operations of that one to one of your VAs and only go back to it once or twice every week.

Learn to cross sell related products

In each of your affiliate marketing websites, you will have one bestselling item. Sometimes, the product that sells best is something that you are not promoting. A scuba diving website for instance may sell more Go Pro accessories than actual scuba gears and equipment. To maximize the growth of these websites, you need to learn about which products are most effective to promote. You also need to learn how to promote related products. When showing a video in your website for instance, you could mention the type of camera that you used to shoot that video and have an affiliate link pointing to that camera in Amazon.

Create a core team to grow your business

The most important part of growing your business is having people around you that you can trust to help you out. As you become more successful, you can hire people to do the work for you. Whether they are virtual assistants or real employees, you should try to keep them if they can do good work.

Each person in your group should play an important role in the group for increasing the income of the business. Keep a core team of great performers and compensate them well so that they will stay with you. You can even take in business partners if they are willing to chip in with the capital of building the business.

Reinvest profits to growing your business

With affiliate marketing, you are using your money to earn more money, especially if you start using paid methods of gaining traffic. In the beginning, the risk is high and there is good chance that some of your ad campaigns will lead to losses. Everything changes however, if you manage to match the right group of people to the right affiliate program. By following the tracking practices discussed in the previous sections, you will be able to make your ads target and reach the right kinds of people.

When you find success with your ad targeting and affiliate program, you should try to maximize profits by increasing the scale of your add campaign. To do this, you will need to reinvest the amount you earn from your affiliate marketing ad campaigns. Use it to fund more ad campaigns or to promote new products to the same audience. If you successfully promoted a camping tent to a group of audience for example, you could cross sell other camping equipment to them. You could then use part of the profits from past campaigns to fund this one.

Renegotiate the terms with the advertiser

If you experience success in promoting a specific product, you may be able to find some leverage to negotiate with the advertisers. You will not be able to do this with big online retailers like Amazon or eBay. However, you may be able to do it with some affiliate networks.

You will be able to contact the advertiser through the support team of the affiliate program. When negotiating, you can ask for special perks that are not available in the regular affiliate marketing program. For example, you can ask for higher commission rates to keep promoting their products. You will need to have a long relationship with the advertiser to be able to ask for something like this. You also should be bringing in a lot of sales for you to be able to demand a pay raise.

You could say for example, that a competing company has contacted you to promote their products and that they are offering a higher commission rate for products of the same price. You could then ask the advertiser if it is possible for them to match the offer.

You could also ask for other types of requests from your advertiser. For example, you could ask for a special promotional coupon that is specific to you website. When a person uses your coupon, the sale is automatically assigned to you. This is a common practice among affiliate marketers who create video content. For this type of affiliate marketers, links are ineffective because they cannot just put links on their videos. YouTube linking features for example, usually do not show in the same way when viewed from mobile phones.

Because of this, many video content creators miss some affiliate sales. Instead of using links to validate a sale, they use coupons because they can mention the coupon code in their videos. The viewers are also likely to use the coupon because it will give them a discount. If you show strong sale numbers, you may be able to ask for this kind of set up from your advertiser.

Don't just create websites, create brands

Your website just serves as the headquarters for an entire network of content marketing assets. The entirety of your online business spreads far beyond the webpages of your website. To make the most of your online assets and all the expenses you put into building and developing it, you should create a brand.

A brand is a business entity that is easily recognizable to the consumers. When your website becomes familiar to the average internet user, you no longer need to write your website name and your tagline for them to know what your website is about. Instead, you only need to show your logo and the visitors will understand what your brand is about. Together with being easily recognized, brands are also associated with certain qualities that are unique to their products, services and company culture.

In the same way, you can also build your website and all your other assets to represent your brand. While your primary method of earning is called affiliate marketing, your business is actually called a content marketing business. With this type of business, you are using your content to drive attention towards your online assets. In the process, you make suggestions in your content that lead to affiliate marketing sales.

A branded content marketing company is not new. All news websites and online magazines are considered content marketing companies. You can also transition your small affiliate marketing website to become a strong content marketing brand. To do this, your audience needs to see positive qualities that they will be able to associate with your brand. Start by making sure that your website and your social media assets are updated in a consistent manner.

You could include a blog in your websites for example, where you talk about tips regarding your affiliate marketing niche. The constant addition of new content will improve your SEO ranking in some keywords. It will also give you something to share organically in your social networking pages. If people expect your website to update regularly, they will remember to go back to it every now and then. While not all of these people will buy from your affiliate links, many of them will help in spreading your content, increasing the reach of each post in your website.

Aside from posting content consistently, you should also aim to continuously improve the quality of your content. If you post spam in your social networking pages, people will associate your brand to spamming. To prevent this from happening, you should only post high quality content in your website. You should not just create and post content for the sake of checking the task off your to-do list. Instead, you should focus on making content because it will be useful to the people who regularly visit your website.

To further establish your brand, you want to maintain a consistent image in all of your online marketing assets. Your logo, name and website tagline should be the same in all these assets including your website, your social media accounts and even your offline presence. The way you talk in these assets should also be the same. If you are using professional English in your website to attract professionals, you should also use the same way of talking in your social media communications. If you choose to make changes in your brand identity (like changing the logo), you should do it simultaneously in all your online assets.

Lastly, the most important quality of a brand is its staying power. Most of us do not actually know how profitable our favorite brands are. Because of this, most people judge whether a brand is successful or not based on its staying power. Brands that still exist are considered strong and those that are becoming less relevant, are considered weak. To establish that your content marketing brand is strong, you should maintain your consistency of posting and creating content. Every now and again, you could create promotions and special events for your readers.

With consistent content creation and marketing, people will look up to your brand as a reliable source of information. If they see your brand's domain name in the search result pages, they are more likely to click on it even if there are other search results entries above yours. They are more likely to trust your content when they see it in their social networking feeds, whether it is in Facebook, Twitter or LinkedIn. Every now and again, they will see your content in apps like Instagram or Pinterest. This may motivate them to give your website a visit. With continued exposure to your content, they will eventually click on your affiliate marketing links when they need the product or services that you are suggesting.

Congratulations!

The sixth character of the password required to unlock the Traffic Optimization Secrets booklet is letter t.

Chapter 12 Quiz
Please refer to Appendix K for the answers to this quiz

1. What can happen if you pose as an expert in a niche you have no experience in that may damage your business?

   A) You will get more sales
   B) People will see you as an expert
   C) Someone may call you out as a fraud
   D) Your brand will look stronger

2. What two activities should you focus on in the beginning of your affiliate marketing career?

   A) Social media marketing and making ads
   B) Gathering traffic and building high quality content
   C) Finding people to work with and passing the work to them
   D) Collecting and sending emails to strangers

3. What is the risk with depending on just one website?

   A) People will not trust your website
   B) You will not have enough domain names for promoting multiple products
   C) People will view your website as amateurish
   D) The business may suffer when the niche market has negative news

4. When negotiating with an affiliate, what should you use as leverage?

   A) Your excellent sales performance
   B) The size of your website
   C) The number of followers you have in Instagram
   D) The number of employees you have

5. What is one factor that makes up the brand identity?

   A) Social media ads
   E) Content length
   F) Website Logo
   G) Website color scheme

6. What make great brands unique from other generic companies?

   A) Unique, recognizable and positive company culture
   B) Low prices

C) High product demand

D) Unique color schemes

7. What is an example of a positive quality that people can associate with a good content marketing brand?

A) High quality content design

B) Video content curation from YouTube

C) Long articles

D) Timely and consistent posting of content

8. What is an example of an activity that can hurt your brand?

A) Creating contents with no videos

B) Posting long articles

C) Posting Spam

D) Removing the comment section

9. Which of the following characteristics contributes to a strong brand image?

A) Removing the comment section in posts

B) Posting memes every day in your website

C) The presence of employees

D) Consistency in website and social media marketing

10. What is the most important brand quality?

A) Staying Power

B) Great Logo

C) Long articles

D) Funny videos

Inspiration #13

"The successful warrior is the average man, with laser-like focus."

Bruce Lee

Chapter 13

Proven Ways to Improve Website Traffic

Success in affiliate marketing can mean earning millions of dollars every month. The very best players in the market achieve this level of earnings on a regular basis. How do you reach this level of success? Check out these tips to start:

Gaining traffic is probably the most difficult part of affiliate marketing. You will need to attract massive numbers of the right types of people to your website. You want the types who are likely to be interested in the products you promote and the content your offer. Here are some of the tested and proven ways of gaining traffic:

Guest posting

This method of getting traffic is one of the most intimidating for most internet marketers. In this section, we will discuss how to do it properly so that you will be able to push through with it.

The first step of guest posting is always to create an excellent article. You want to write content on something that you are confident writing about. You want to write about something that is related to the topic of your affiliate website.

When creating the content that you will offer for guest posting, you will need to make sure that it is well researched and it is pleasant to read to the readers of the other website. The readers will judge you based on the quality of content that you will share. If they like your content, they may go to your website and check out your other articles. If they do not like your content, they may ignore you, or worse, talk about how bad your content is in the comments.

After creating the new content, it's time to look for a website where you will share it. To begin with, make a list of websites where some of your target audiences may regularly visit. Ideally, it should not be another affiliate marketing website. Instead, find websites that are considered as authorities in your niche industry.

One option is to approach real world publications and offer your services as a freelancer. You can find a write-for-us section in websites like the Huffington Post or Bleacher Report. These popular website get thousands of requests from aspiring writers every day. You do not want to go after these general publications. Instead, you should focus on the big publications or online magazines that cater to your niche.

Make a list of at least twenty of these online publications. After creating the list, you will need to contact these companies to ask if you can write in their website. To achieve this, you will need to email the administrators of the websites. Most of them have a contact-us page or a write-for-us page. Do not expect that you will be compensated in any way for your guest posting. You will need to do this service for free.

In your email, be courteous and go straight to the point. You could use the same emails for all your applications, changing only small details. In the email, you could provide a link back to your website so that they will be able to see samples of the articles you have written. This will allow them to inspect your content easily, giving them an idea of the type of content that you can share in their website.

If you have confidence that the content you created will stand out and increase the chance that your offer will be approved, you could also mention it in the email. You could talk about what the content is about and how it can be valuable to their website.

If you hear back from them, you may need to ask for the terms of the partnership. In exchange for writing for their website, you need to ask to have a link back to your own website. The link will help your own website in terms of search engine ranking. If the website you will be writing for has a strong marketing arm, you may even get some traffic from the link.

If you are accepted and you agree on the terms of the guest posting, you will be asked to submit a file of the article that you will post. In most cases, the administrators of the website will have suggestions on how you will change the content. The changes are not always significant. They will mostly be done to make your content fit the other types of content in their website.

After some editing, your content will be posted in their website and you may see some traffic come out of it. Make sure though that the terms that were agreed upon are followed. Your name should be mentioned as the author of the content and there should be a link going back to your affiliate website. If there is no traffic surge to your website, you will still get some SEO juice from the link in your content. Once your guest post is up, do not think too much about it. The content is there for everyone to see. If the website has a strong SEO presence, you may have your guest post rank well.

Now that you are done, you should shift your focus on working on a new guest post. You should do one of these guest posts a month. The overall goal is to increase the number of contents you have from other websites. With each guest post you set up, you will get a legitimate backlink to your own website and you may get some traffic.

Some of your contents will be more successful than others. If you see that one of your articles get a lot of attention in one website, you can ask the administrators if they would like you to do another one. You should do this for the websites where your guest posts get a lot of positive results like great search ranking and a high number of referred traffic.

Guesting on a Vlog

Guesting opportunities online do not only apply to online articles. They can also be applied in podcasts and in vlogs. You could follow the same strategy discussed above to book other promotional events. For instance, you could message a YouTube channel manager if you could talk in one of their shows or if they would like you to become a guest in their shows.

If you have a tech website for instance, you could ask to guest in tech shows and news websites. You could also look for podcasts about your topic. The best part about this type of guesting is that you get your name and your work out there without the need for excessive preparations. This allows you to reserve your writing talents to your own contents. Becoming a guest in internet shows can be fun and it does not take a lot of work.

You do not have to travel to the exact place of the vlogger either. You can set up your own working place so that it is suitable for internet videos. News agencies use skype all the time to talk to their guests in the show. You and the vlogger can also do this. This way, it will not cost you much to appear in the shows of other influencers in your circles.

To become a guest, you will need to meet in person or virtually with the vlogger and review what you will talk about in the show. Most vloggers will only invite you in their shows if you are already an established expert in your niche and your inputs in the show matches the needs of their audience.

Search Engine Optimization

The best way to get traffic to your website is through search engine optimization. Search engines are the primary tools used by internet users to get around online. Unlike social media, these tools are used not just for entertainment and communication. They are used to look for specific types of content in the searchable web. Search engines "crawl" and collect information all public websites online. They organize the websites based on the data they collect about it. Mostly, they are concerned with the information found in the website. However, they also collect information related to user experience such as website speed, server uptime and the presence of malware or other dangerous types of codes.

If your website is found to be safe, legal, and easy to use, it will be added to the search database. To match the information in your website the needs of internet users, Google and other search engines use keywords and phrases.

When the internet user enters a word or phrase in the search bar, the search algorithm uses this information and searches all the websites they've crawled for matching information. Because multiple websites have the same type of information, reaching the top spot of the list in the search result pages will require you to deal with intense competition, especially in the most popular topics.

If you do manage to outrank all the other pages in your niche topic, you will manage to attract the people in your niche market. This type of traffic is considered by most affiliate marketers to be superior in quality compared to the ones coming from social networks because they are using the internet to deal with a specific need. If you happen to have the solution to their needs, you can earn by suggesting affiliate products to them.

How to optimize content for search engines

Search engine marketing comes in many phases. The first phase starts in the building and development of your website. In this part of the process, you need to decide on the identity of your website. To establish your website's identity, the search engines will check factors like your domain name, your website tag line and the different internal links (links that lead to other pages inside the same website) you offer in your website's primary menu. Secondary to this, your website identity will be determined by the headlines of your posts.

Ideally, these headlines should have an H1 tag. Ideally, you should start adding the most important keywords in your niche at this part of the process. If possible, you can include your keyword and phrase in the domain name. You should also use related keywords and phrases in the relevant links in your website, especially the ones in your menus. This makes up the basic parts of your site-level optimization.

The second phase of search engine marketing involves page-level optimization. This is the more crucial part of the two because it will be your pages that will be individually ranked in the search result pages. It all starts with the keywords you use in the title of your article. Ideally, the keywords or phrases should be placed in the beginning of the headline. Also make sure that the title includes 50-60 characters only. Google displays this range of characters in the search results.

Next to the title, you should also consider what to write in the meta description of the page. The meta description is the paragraph that will be used below the SEO title. This part should help establish the information in the page to the internet user. You do not have to overthink this part. Just tell the reader, in a conversational manner, what information is included in the page. Ideally, you should make this paragraph be around 320 characters long. You should also include the relevant keywords or phrase in this paragraph.

Next, you will need to create the body of your content. From an SEO standpoint, the body should be at least 350 words long for short content types like news, blog posts and updates. For posts that require instructions and steps, the word count should be north of 750 words to be competitive. The text components of the body should include paragraphs (with a <p> tag) and headings (h2, h3…). You should mention the keyword or phrase multiple times in the paragraphs. It should also be included in at least two paragraph headings.

If the content is intended to show a process, like how-to contents, you will need to use the list tags (<ol> or <ul>). This will tell the search engines that you are presenting a list to the intended audience. Aside from using the list content as your paragraph headings, you should also include multiple types of media to make the content easier for the eyes.

The first type of media that you should add is the text. The text portion of the content is easy to optimize for the search engine because you can simply write the keywords and phrases as they are needed in the paragraphs.

Ideally, the keywords and phrases should comprise 1-2% of your text content. The first one should be included within the first two sentences of the first paragraph. If you have a 1,000-word long article, you should use your keyword or phrase ten to twenty times. You should not allow the content however, to contain more that 4% of the keyword or phrase. More than that, Google may flag you for keyword stuffing. This may have your content penalized for gaming the search engine algorithm.

Next to text, the second most important type of content is the image. The presence of images in the page indicates a break in the wall of text content. By breaking the content into chunks with the use of images, you will make your content easier for the eyes of the user. To make the images help in your SEO efforts, you should include the keyword or phrase in the alt-attribute of the image. In most website content management systems, the option to change the alt-attribute is present when the image is uploaded or edited. Adding a caption also helps to establish the nature of the image.

Lastly, you will need to add a video whenever there is a need for it. The video should complement the content of the website. Of the three types of content discussed in this section, you should be least worried with optimizing the video content. Focus your SEO on the other two types of content.

With these three types of contents, you will be able to establish what the page is about. The next step is to use links to establish how it relates to the other contents in the web. Links come in two types, inbound links and outbound links. You could use your outbound links to link to other pages that may be useful the user. You should do this when the linked page has information that is not included in your own page. The links in your page are either internal (going to other pages in the same website) or external (going to pages of other websites). Feel free to use internal links as you see fit.

However, you should be more careful when linking externally. Make sure that the third party website that you are linking to is safe to use and hosts legal contents. Ideally, the page you are linking to should be related to the topic that you are talking about in the page. Linking to other websites is supposed to supplement the knowledge of the user about the topic. The search engine crawlers (robots that check your website) will use the content that you are using to guess what type of content your website has.

Linking externally should be done naturally. If you mentioned a technical term that a few people may not understand for example, you can add a link to a page with the definition of the said word. Adding the right links is important in affiliate marketing. By making your readers become accustomed to the use of links, you may increase the chances of clicks to the affiliate text links you add to your content.

Now, let's talk about the SEO functions of inbound links. Inbound links are used by the search engine algorithm as a metric for how popular and useful a website is. Inbound links refer to the links from other websites that lead to the webpages in your website. You can use tools like the Google Search Console (sometimes also called Google Webmaster Tools) to check which websites are linking to your pages.

Each link that points to your webpages has a different value. The search engine ranking algorithm considers factors like the age of the domain, its Page Rank and many other different metrics to decide whether a link adds value to the webpage it is pointing to. Many online marketers for instance, believe that links from difficult to obtain domains like the ones with a .gov or .edu extensions are more valuable than those from .com domains.

There are multiple legal ways for you to get inbound links to your webpage. The first one is to do your professional networking in your industry. If you are in the gardening industry for example, you should look for other webmasters in the same industry. Links from their websites or blogs will tell the search engines that your webpages are also about gardening. If most of your links are coming from US based websites with US-centric contents, this will also signal that your content is also for US audiences.

Aside from obtaining links from the websites of people you know, you could also get them by doing guest posting. This is the reason why you really need to negotiate to have a link pointing back to your website every time you do your guest posting. As suggested in the guest posting section of this book, you should choose the websites that you guest post to. They should be related to your niche, they should have access to a market that does not currently go to your website, and they should have a good search rankings. It is ideal if you could get your guest posts from websites with better search engine rankings in keywords that you are interested to compete in.

Marketing in forums and other online communities

Aside from social networks and the search engines, you will need to work with other types of websites that have a big online community. To do this, you will need to look for the types of websites where your average target audience spends a lot of his in. This could be a forum, a membership website or an online app.

If this website has lots of contents, you could also ask to guest post in it. Some blogs for example, has a high following of people that post a lot of comments. With this type of blog, the community it mostly concentrated in the comment section. You may use this section of the website to communicate with your prospect website visitors. Ideally, you should add useful comments in this section to answer other commenters' questions. You could then suggest links for suggested sources of information. In the process, you could also add your own content in here.

Forums are also great sources of traffic. However, forum members tend to be avid internet users. Because of this, they are warry about salesy people online. Before you can convince others to go to your website, you should first gain their trust. In the forum culture, this usually means that you need to contribute content to the forum while following the forum rules. Many forums have point and ranking systems. Active members tend to get more points, increasing their ranking in the website. This gives them certain perks that less active members do not have.

When you have developed a strong relationship with the people in the forums, you can now start promoting your own content. Even if you are already a trusted member in the forum, you should still only suggest your content in the context of the conversation in the forums.

You could also consider looking for Q&A websites. Websites like Quora and the once popular Yahoo Answers, are examples of websites like these. Q&A sites can either be general, like in the case of Quora, or specific. Specific Q&A websites allow only answers related to the topic. There are some Q&A websites for example that focuses on questions related to solving Windows Personal Computer problems. If your content is related to solving PC problems, this may be a good community for you to work with. There are also some that only allow questions about fitness. You will need to find a Q&A website that fits your niche. Only work with it if it has an active community. You can check this out by going straight to their website and checking out the website activity.

Using ads to get traffic

When your website is ready to accept traffic, it's time to start use paid methods to pump traffic into it. It is common to make the mistake of relying solely on organic means of getting traffic. This process takes too long. Let's say you work hard to build your content base and your social media presence. After your done setting everything up for getting organic traffic, the newsfeeds algorithm changes for Facebook, making all your previous efforts futile. A similar event happened to many affiliate marketers back when Google launched its Panda and Penguin updates. The majority of people who depended only on organic traffic were affected the most when pages were penalized.

To learn why you need to use paid means of getting traffic, let us first discuss the differences between free and paid traffic.

Free versus paid traffic

As mentioned above, free traffic is known in the industry as organic traffic. Any visitor coming to your website because of your free efforts in social media and search engine optimization can be considered organic. In the beginning, this will be your primary source of traffic. In fact, it is highly encouraged by affiliate marketing experts that you master the skill of gaining free traffic first.

Free traffic however, is harder to get than most beginners think. The first big factor that works against free traffic is competition. Regardless of what niche topic you choose, there will always be people who will be competing with you. They will compete with you in competing for the attention of your target audience.

If you are promoting a special type of food supplement in your website for example, there will be other people who will be promoting the same product. And you are trying to attract, the same group of people that you are attracting. In the online world, it is easy to track what your competition is doing. You simply go to their websites or their Facebook pages to see what type of promotions they are running. When you become successful, you should expect that your competitors will also be doing the same thing.

With paid traffic, there will also be some competition. However, the number of competing websites will not be as high those competing in free traffic channels. In most websites, there is usually a place for ads, separated from the other types of content. In Google's search result pages for example, the ads are usually located at the top part of the search results. Before the organic search results, you will see two to four ads placements first. Because it is seen first by the search engine user, they are likely to click on it first.

The second big factor to consider when deciding whether to use paid traffic sources, is the speed of business progress. Because of the high level of competition with organic marketing methods, it usually takes an affiliate websites some time before a significant amount of traffic starts coming in. This can be a problem for affiliate marketers with a small capital. The sales come with the traffic that you funnel towards your website. The more traffic comes in, the higher the chances of sales will be. In the beginning, you will only get between 0-10 people coming into your website daily if you rely only on passive and organic means. This is the amount of traffic that you should expect if you are only adding one article in your website and posting one or two contents in your social media channels per day.

The amount of traffic that you get through organic means depends on the number of users you can reach in social media and your search ranking in Google. In the beginning, you will not fare well in both of these marketing factors. With less than 10 people coming to your website daily, you cannot expect to get a substantial income from your affiliate website.

Paid campaigns enhance organic marketing efforts

You should not approach your paid campaigns as separate from your organic marketing efforts. Any success you experience with your paid marketing will also trickle down towards your organic marketing channels. If you make a Facebook ad for instance, some people who do not click on your ads may choose to click on your page and follow it, instead. Some people who do not click on your call to action button in your landing page may choose to surf around your website and they may choose to return at a later date. While behaviors like these do not show as a success in your ad campaign tracking tools, they still have a positive effect on your business.

Using Ads to Get Traffic

Getting few daily visits does not mean that your business model will not work. It just means that you are not getting enough traffic to make the system work. It also means that you are not reaching your target audience with the organic traffic marketing that you are using. You will eventually reach these people with organic marketing methods however, it may take you years to reach your goal.

There are multiple ways to get the amount of traffic that you want. However, the best and fastest way it so use paid methods. Using this method can be risky, especially if you do not know what you are doing. The risk is highest in the beginning when you have no experience of using the advertising platform. You can prepare for your first marketing campaign as much as you can through books and YouTube tutorials but you will learn most of the best practices in marketing with experience. Even if you have decided to use ads to drive traffic to your website, there will still be a lot of planning needed to make sure that you succeed in carrying out an effective and efficient campaign.

First, you need to choose a platform where you will use ads. There are various online platforms to choose from including Facebook Advertising and Google AdWords. These two are probably the biggest mainstream advertising platforms and they are the most recommended for beginners. These two stand out because of the number of people that their platforms can reach. Google AdWords can be used to create ads for search engine result pages, websites using Google AdSense and apps that are using mobile AdSense ads. If your marketing message is better delivered using videos, you can also use AdWords to put up ads in YouTube.

You can target your ads based on the search terms used by people. Text and banner ads shown in website hosting AdSense can be targeted using the type of content in the said website and the information that Google has on the person using the website. For instance, you can make your ads appear only in financial websites to promote your financial affiliate programs. You can also make the ad target market narrower by targeting people only from specific countries.

With mobile becoming the primary way of using Google, the AdWords platform also allows advertisers to target users based on the type of device they are using. If the product you are promoting can only be used through mobile, you can make your ads show only on mobile devices.

Most importantly, Google has a variety of free tools that allows you to monitor and learn from your ad campaigns. For instance, you can use Google Analytics to track the number of visits you get from an ad campaign. With this tool, you can also use this tool to track how these people moved around your website and whether they clicked on any of your affiliate links or not.

Facebook Ads on the other hand standout because of the wealth of information that Facebook has about their users. Just like Google AdWords, Facebook ads can also be used to target people based on the device and the type of network they are using (Wi-Fi or mobile data). The primary types of information used targeting in Facebook though are the person's interests and basic demographics. Basic demographics refer to information like the person's age, gender, location and occupation. Facebook allows advertisers to use these types of information for ad targeting. Advertisers can then use the person's interests to make the targeting narrower. The interests of a person are based on the contents that they engaged with in the network. A person who follows basketball stars and teams for example, will be matched with ads that are targeted to people who are interested in basketball. That pretty much sums up the basic way of ad targeting in Facebook.

Tracking success and refining your campaigns

Your success in affiliate marketing will depend on how you adjust your ad campaigns to make them more effective and efficient. To do this, you will need to use two important tools. The first one is Google Analytics. This tool will tell you how people arrived in your website, what pages they viewed while they were there and on what page they left. If the visitor viewed more than one webpage, additional information like the average time spent on the website will be available.

You can use Google Analytics to decide whether your ads campaign is bringing enough traffic or not. You can also use it to track the movements of your users within your website. Most importantly, you can use this tool to check whether the users you've targeted click on your affiliate links or not.

The next best tool for tracking your ad campaigns is Facebook Pixels. Similar to Google Analytics, Facebook Pixels requires that you use a tracking code in your website. With this tracking code, you will be able to track the website users who come from Facebook. By tracking these people, you will be able to create a custom audience made up of Facebook users who go to your website. By using this feature, you will be able to create ads targeted towards people who are already visitors of your website.

For example, you could create a page that will redirect people to the landing pages of the affiliate link. You could then use Facebook Pixel to track this page. Next, you will need to distribute a link to this page around the website, which will serve as your proxy affiliate link. You should promote this link as you would promote your affiliate website. When people from Facebook click on that link, they will be redirected to the affiliate landing page. But before that, they will first pass through the proxy page, allowing Facebook Pixel to track their activity. Back in Facebook Pixels, you can create a Custom Audience made up of only those people who clicked on that link. This way, you will be able to create ads or boosted Facebook content specifically targeted towards people who clicked on your Facebook link in the past.

Another feature unique to Facebook ads is the ability to create a Lookalike Audience. This type of audience is created by using the qualities of a previous group you've created. Let's say you have a Facebook page with 100 likes. You want to increase the number of likes to your page using a Facebook promotion. You can create the Lookalike Audience feature to target people who are similar to the people who liked your page.

You could also make a Lookalike Audience group from the data you've gathered from Facebook Pixels. First, you will need to set up Facebook Pixels in the pages that you want to track. Next, you will need to create a custom audience made up of people who visited the page tracked by Facebook Pixel. Lastly, you can create a Lookalike Audience based on the custom audience group you've created. The people in the Lookalike Audience group will be new users who have similar characteristics of people who clicked your affiliate link. This type of audience is likely to click on your affiliate links in the future.

While this all sounds great in theory, the reality is that it will take you multiple tries to create the best type of audience group in your Facebook ad campaign. Even if you already have a successful campaign, you should not stop tracking. Keep tracking your campaigns and making adjustments. You should then test these adjustments to keep improving your ads targeting system.

Starting your first campaign

An ad campaign will only become successful if you do the necessary preparations before you start doing it. Follow these steps to increase the likelihood of success in your first campaigns:

Define your advertising goal

All your decisions and the actions you make should be based on one advertising goal. In most cases, your goal will be related to increasing sales. For instance, you could create a goal of sending more traffic towards a specific affiliate link.

Identify the target audience of your advertising

The next step is to identify the types of people you need to reach. You need to create a profile of your target audience based on the affiliate product that you are promoting. If you are promoting a high-end electronic shaver for example, your target will be men who are obsessed with grooming. If you are promoting luxury handbags on the other hand, your target will be women who are interested in fashion and luxury items.

To begin with, try to think of real people you know who are interested in the product you are promoting. Using these people as your inspiration, try to identify the defining characteristics of your target audience. You should include basic information like age, gender and location. You could also include specific information like interests and preferences of the people you are targeting. For example, you can target people with specific hobbies or with important responsibilities.

Identify the platform where you will put your ads

You do not have to create ads in all of the advertising platforms online. This will cost a lot of money. Instead, you should only look for the platform where your target audiences are found. If your target users are searching for the product online, you can choose to use Google AdWords so that your ad will be shown in the search result pages. On the other hand, if the product you are promoting is visually appealing, you can put your ads in highly visual social networks like Instagram, YouTube or Pinterest.

If you are targeting professionals, you could use networks that can target this kind of information. LinkedIn and Facebook for instance are able to group people based on their occupation. You could use these networks to target people of specific professions.

If you are just targeting anyone from a specific location, you also have the option to use CPM advertising. CPM or cost per mille is an advertising scheme where in the advertisers pay per 1000 impressions on an ad. With this type of advertising scheme, you will be able to show your ads to thousands of people. The targeting tools of this kind of advertising are less accurate than that used in Google and Facebook ads. This is more suited for affiliate marketers who are offering products with no specific target buyers in mind.

After choosing your advertising platform, you should learn as much as you can about it before making your first ad campaign. You could begin by reading about how others experienced creating their first campaigns. You can go online to learn about how to do a campaign.

After learning how to do it through people's blog posts, you can learn further by making a mock campaign. Go to your chosen ad platform, create an account and test out their interface on creating your first campaign. You will not be charged until the ad goes live.

Create a plan for the overall user experience

Before you make your first campaign, you should first plan what kind of user experience you will give your audience. In this step, you should draw up how you will make use of the traffic that you will get from the ad. If the affiliate program will allow you, you can make the traffic go straight to the affiliate link's landing page to minimize the chance that the visitor will bounce. Many affiliate programs allow this kind of traffic scheme however, they do specify not to use ad keywords that may compete with their own ads. An affiliate program for a website called ABC.com for example, will usually not allow you to use the words ABC.com. If you choose to use this path, you should use a redirect page to go between the ads and the affiliate landing page. This will allow you to track the number of users that your ad brings to the link. It also allows you to use Google Analytics and Facebook Pixel to track the users.

If the affiliate program does not allow ad traffic, you can still make use of ads. However, you will need to send them to your own website first. If the ad link goes directly to the affiliate landing page, the ad only needs one click for it to be successful. If you need to make them pass through your website on the other hand, you will need to get an extra click from the users to make the ad successful. First, they need to press the ad link and then, then will need to press the affiliate link on the website. To make this ad scheme successful, you will need to create a great landing page in your website that will receive the traffic sent by the ad.

Create your advertising creatives

Now that you have chosen the platform where you will publish your ads, the next step is to create the creatives or visual marketing materials. First, you will need to decide on the type of ad that you will use. Search result pages only allow text ads to show while Facebook allows a combination of image and texts. Ads for mobile are also mostly just text ads while ads published in websites are mostly in the form of banners.

After deciding on a type of creative, it is time make them. Text ads are the easiest to create because they do not need an image to become live. You only need to decide on what your ad will say and then input the statements in the ad creation process. Text ads in the internet usually come in a specific format. The biggest part of the ad is the title and it states what the ad is offering the online user. Below it, there is usually subtitle in smaller fonts. This part explains further the offer made in the title of the ad. Lastly, the last part of the ad is the URL or Domain name where the ad will go when someone clicks on it. Text ads are usually used by cost per click networks like Google AdWords.

Next to text, the second type of ad contains images. These are more commonly known as banner ads because they are usually square or rectangles in spaces around the content. You can create them yourself using Adobe Photoshop or any other image editing tool. You can also use free tools like Canva.com to craft it. If you do not want to make your own ad creatives, you can choose to have it made with websites like Fiverr.com.

When creating ad images, make sure that the offer is clear by adding text over the image. Remember to state a clear offer to the intended audience. With the fewest number of words possible, tell the target audience what you are offering or what problem you are trying to solve. You can use a straight statement that says what product or service you are offering or you can start the ad text with a question. Also include the name of your website. This way, you will be putting the name of your website out there.

With images, you can add whatever you want in the ad. However, ad images with people tend to have better click-through rates than those that only contain images of things. However, there is no way of knowing the effectiveness of an ad image for sure before launching it. The best strategy is to try out multiple images and track the methods of each.

Create a landing page

Next to the contents of the ads, the landing page is the most important part of the entire ad process. If the landing page is convincing, the entire user experience that comes with the ad will convert a high percentage of visitors. Otherwise, the ad campaign will lead to losses.

When creating a landing page, think of how you can convince the ad visitor to buy the product. This usually begins with a description of the product and statement of the benefits that comes with using the product or service. Ideally, you should also add features like testimonials from other users of the product as well as video reviews showing people using the product or service.

Throughout the page, there should be a call-to-action button with the affiliate link. The call to action button usually comes with a text component. Many affiliate marketers use words like "Buy Now" or "Visit Website". Make sure to modify the words that you use here so that they catch the eye of the visitor. You could also test different colors of the call to action button or link. Together with the call-to-action button, you should also include a short descriptive paragraph that tells the users what to expect when they click on the button. By adding this paragraph, you are making the process of going to the website of the user easier for the visitor. Most people try to avoid buttons when they do not know what it does. By explaining what the button does, you will be able to set the right expectations to the prospect buyer.

Just like your ad text and images, you should also try out multiple ad landing pages to see which ones are most effective. You could changes different factors to see how they perform when traffic passes through them. You can change the words that you use in the landing page. You could also change other factors like the images and color scheme of the page. After experimenting and getting enough data, stick to the landing pages with the highest success rate.

Remove distractions from landing page

The average webpage has between 30-40 links, going to various pages inside and outside of the website. You should remove these links from your landing pages. The only links in your landing page should be your affiliate link. You should also remove any other distraction that has nothing to do with the product or service that you are offering in the page.

By removing other distractions from the page, you will be able to prevent the user from doing any other action other than to click on the affiliate link in the call-to-action buttons.

Emphasize the benefits of your products by telling a story

The most successful affiliate marketers are master storytellers. They use their storytelling skills to establish the importance of the product they are using. Marketers like Darren Rowse and Pat Flynn for example, use the storytelling method to tell audience about their online projects. In the process, they also talk about what products they use and how these products help them in reaching their goals.

By using storytelling to talk about products and services, marketers are able to connect with the audience without sounding like they are selling something. You can also do this with the products you are using. Instead of just making a list of the benefits of the product for example, you could talk about how you discovered the product. You could also talk about your contrasting experiences before and after using the product. For example, you could talk about how bad your experience was before you discovered the product. You could then explain what the differences were when you started using the product. Your story will have more credibility if you show an image of yourself with the product.

When you run out of stories to tell, tell other people's stories

There will come a time when you exhaust most of your own stories. While they will still be in the internet for new fans to see, you will need to keep serving new content to keep people coming back to your content. To do this, you could discover other people's stories in your niche. Let's say that you have an affiliate website that promotes fitness products. You started your website by talking about how you personally lost weight and started a healthy lifestyle. A year after creating your website, you are running out of things to say about your personal journey. You know that if you stop making content, the traffic will begin to dwindle, decreasing the earning potential of your website.

To be able to create more content, you could look for other people who are undergoing the same journey. You could ask them if they would like to be featured in your website. You could do it in a form of an interview so that you will be able get answers for the important questions. For example, you could look for gym trainers and tell their story in their website. They could talk about their experience in the fitness industry and provide tips to people who are trying to lose weight. You could also talk about the products and services that they would recommend. You could then post an affiliate link of these products.

By creating the stories of other people related to your industry, you will be able to help them promote their own businesses. You will also be able to tap their market when the people you feature share the content about them in their personal social media accounts.

Do the math to check the profitability of an ad

Before you actually launch your first ad campaign, you should first check the cost and reward aspects of the ad. You will need to learn how many sales you will need to make in the particular campaign to break even. If you begin by creating an ad campaign with a $100 budget for example and you get $5 for each sale you create for the affiliate marketer, this means that you will need at least 20 sales to break even. You can lessen the required number of sales that you need to deliver by promoting products with a higher commission. Ideally, you want to increase the commission with products with better commission rates rather than promoting more expensive products. An ad with the same budget but pays out $20 per sale will only require you to make 5 sales to break even. All your sales after the fifth sale will go directly to your profits.

After learning how many sales you need to make, you can run a small scale campaign to test the conversion rates of your content. For example, you can start promoting an affiliate link with a $20 budget in your chosen ad platform. If the ad conversion rate in the $20 campaign looks promising, you could go on with a full scale campaign by increasing the budget or the duration of the ad. Let's say that a $20 campaign brought you 100 visitors and 2 conversions. If each sale makes a $10 revenue, then the ad campaign will just breakeven.

In this case, you need to make some changes to increase the conversion rate of your overall user experience. One thing you can do is to change the ad targeting. You will need to use the tracking tools discussed above to find targeting mistakes that may be affecting the success rates of your ads. You could also check the landing pages of your ads as well as the landing page of the advertiser. Some landing pages for example, use call-to-action buttons that are too small. Sometimes, these buttons may also be in the wrong color or the text included in them may not be inviting enough to click. These factors need to be changed to increase the likelihood of success. Make sure that the call-to-action button is always visible to the audience. Also make changes with the text in the button. Sometimes changing the call-to-action button from "Buy Now" to "Check Prices" may increase the click-through rate of your page.

Chapter 13 Quiz
Please refer to Appendix L for the answers to this quiz

1. How will you be paid for your guest posts?

   A) Guest posting does not pay
   B) Based on the number of words
   C) Based on the amount of traffic that your content gets
   D) Through affiliate sales generated by the guest post

2. What page should you use to contact a website administrator?

   A) Front Page
   B) Exit Page
   C) Contact Us Page
   D) Blog Page

3. What is one positive effect of guest posting?

   A) Positive SEO effects due to backlinks
   B) Increase in popularity
   C) Social Media popularity
   D) More sales

4. What do you call video journal entries in websites like YouTube?

   A) Vines
   B) Skype
   C) Vlog
   D) Blog

5. What tools can you use to become a vlog guest without going to the studios of vloggers?

   A) Skype
   B) Telephone
   C) Audio Recorder
   D) Text-to-Speech Technology

6. What is the biggest search engine in the world?

   A) Google
   B) Yahoo
   C) Amazon

D) Bing

7. What do you call the artificial intelligence software used by search engines to collect information about websites around the web?

   A) Search Engine Crawler
   B) Sear
   C) Search AI
   D) Search Engine Bug

8. What is one factor that establishes your website's identity to search engines?

   A) Social Media Profile Links
   B) Video Content
   C) Color Scheme
   D) Domain Name

9. What do you call the second phase of SEO wherein you optimize each article in your website?

   A) Page-level SEO
   B) Site-level
   C) Site Mapping
   D) Search Analytics

10. What do you call the practice of using keywords and phrases unnaturally in an article in the hopes of ranking higher in search engine results?

    A) Crawling
    B) Keyword Splicing
    C) Keyword Stuffing
    D) Search Engine Optimization

Inspiration #14

"Success seems to be connected with action. Successful people keep moving. They make mistakes, but they don't quit."

Conrad Hilton

Conclusion
Thank you again for downloading this book!

I want to share with you something that I find terribly sad. Once people start reading a book, they typically only read 10 percent of it before they give up or forget about it. Only 10 percent.

What's sad about this is that from this statistic, we can see that very few people actually follow through on what they commit to (at least when it comes to reading). The reason for this is harsh but understandable: most people are not willing to hold themselves accountable. People "want" and "want" all day, but very few actually have the fortitude to put in the work.

So what's my point? First, I am trying to tell you that if you're reading these words, you are a statistical anomaly (and I am grateful for you). But here's the kicker: in order to become successful as a result of this book, you are going to have to be in the .1 percent. You need to take action.

I hope that this book was able to teach you how the affiliate marketing business works and how you can start building your Affiliate marketing business today. The next step is to look into the niche that you would like to take part in and the products that you would like to promote.

Remember that affiliate marketing is all about reaching out to as many people as you can who need the product you promote. If you begin with the right mindset and strategy, there is no doubt that you will succeed in building your affiliate marketing business.

Start by creating one asset at a time and do not give up. The more time and effort you put into this business, the better your chances of succeeding will be. I wish you the very best of luck

The End

Thank you very much for taking the time to read this book. I tried my best to cover as much as I could. If you found it useful please let me know by leaving a review on Amazon! Your support really does make a difference and I read all the reviews personally so I can get your feedback and make this book even better.

I also pride myself on giving my readers the best information out there, being super responsive to them and providing the best customer service. If you feel I have fallen short of this standard in any way, please kindly email me at **michael@michaelezeanaka.com** so I can get a chance to make it right to you. I wish you all the best with your journey towards financial freedom!

Affiliate Marketing: Learn How to Make...
Michael Ezeanaka

Book(s) By Michael Ezeanaka

Affiliate Marketing: Learn How to Make $10,000+ Each Month On Autopilot

Are you looking for an online business that you can start today? Do you feel like no matter how hard you try - you never seem to make money online? If so, this book has you covered. If you correctly implement the strategies in this book, you can make commissions of up to $10,000 (or more) per month in extra income.

- WITHOUT creating your own products
- WITHOUT any business or management experience
- WITHOUT too much start up capital or investors
- WITHOUT dealing with customers, returns, or fulfillment
- WITHOUT building websites
- WITHOUT selling anything over the phone or in person
- WITHOUT any computer skills at all
- WITHOUT leaving the comfort of your own home

In addition, because I enrolled this book in the kindle matchbook program, **Amazon will make the kindle edition available to you for FREE** after you purchase the paperback edition from Amazon.com, saving you roughly $6.99!!

Available In Kindle, Paperback and **Audio**

Passive Income Ideas: 50 Ways To Make Money Online Analyzed

How many times have you started a business only to later realise it wasn't what you expected? Would you like to go into business knowing beforehand the potential of the business and what you need to do to scale it? If so, this book can help you

In Passive Income Ideas, you'll discover

- A concise, step-by-step analysis of **50 business models** you can leverage to earn passive income (Including one that allows you to earn money watching TV!)
- Strategies that'll help you greatly simplify some of the business models (and in the process **make them more passive!**)
- What you can do to scale your earnings (regardless of which business you choose)
- Strategies you can implement to **minimize the level of competition** you face in each marketplace
- Myths that tend to hold people back from succeeding in their business (**we debunk more than 100 such myths!**)
- Well over 150 Insightful tips that'll give you an edge and help you succeed in whichever business you chose to pursue
- More than 100 frequently asked questions (**with answers**)

- 50 positive vitamins for the mind (in the form of inspirational quotes that'll keep you going during the tough times)
- A business scorecard that neatly summarizes, in alphabetical order, each business models score across 4 criteria i.e. simplicity, passivity, scalability and competitiveness
- …and much much more!

What's more? Because the book is enrolled in kindle matchbook program, **Amazon will make the kindle edition available to you for FREE** after you purchase the paperback edition from Amazon.com, saving you roughly $6.99!!

Available In Kindle, Paperback and **Audio**

Work From Home: 50 Ways To Make Money Online Analyzed

This is a **2-in-1 book bundle** consisting of the below books. Amazon will make the kindle edition available to you for FREE when you purchase the print version of this bundle from Amazon.com - **saving you roughly 35%** from the price of the individual books.

- Passive Income Ideas – 50 Ways to Make Money Online Analyzed (Part I)
- Affiliate Marketing – Learn How to Make $10,000+ Each Month on Autopilot (Part 2)

Get this bundle at a 35% discount from Amazon.com

Available In Kindle, Paperback and **Audio**

Dropshipping: Discover How to Make Money Online, Build Sustainable Streams of Passive Income and Gain Financial Freedom Using The Dropshipping E-Commerce Business Model

How many times have you started a business only to later realise you had to spend a fortune to get the products manufactured, hold inventory and eventually ship the products to customers all over the globe?

Would you like to start your very own e-commerce business that gets right to making money without having to deal with all of these issues? If so, this book can help you

In this book, you'll discover:

- A simple, step-by-step explanation of what the dropshipping business is all about (**Chapter 1**)
- 8 reasons why you should build a dropshipping business (**Chapter 2**)
- Disadvantages of the dropshipping business model and what you need to look out for before making a decision (**Chapter 3**)

- How to start your own dropshipping business including the potential business structure to consider, how to set up a company if you're living outside the US, how much you'll need to start and sources of funding (**Chapter 4**)
- How the supply chain and fulfilment process works – illustrated with an example transaction (**Chapter 5**)
- Analysis of 3 potential sales channel for your dropshipping business - including their respective pros and cons (**Chapter 6**)
- How to do niche research and select winning products – including the tools you need and where to get them (**Chapter 7**)
- How to find reliable suppliers and manufacturers. As well as 6 things you need to look out for in fake suppliers (**Chapter 8**)
- How to manage multiple suppliers and the inventory they hold for you (**Chapter 9**)
- How to deal with security and fraud issues (**Chapter 10**)
- What you need to do to minimize chargebacks i.e. refund rates (**Chapter 11**)
- How to price accordingly especially when your supplier offers international shipment (**Chapter 12**)
- 10 beginner mistakes and how to avoid them (**Chapter 13**)
- 7 powerful strategies you can leverage to scale up your dropshipping business (**Chapter 14**)
- 15 practical tips and lessons from successful dropshippers (**Chapter 15**)

And much, much more!

Finally, because this book is enrolled in Kindle Matchbook Program, the **kindle edition of this book will be available to you for free** when you purchase the paperback version from Amazon.com.

If you're ready to take charge of your financial future, grab your copy of this book today! Start taking control of your life by learning how to create a stream of passive income that'll take care of you and your loved ones.

Available In Kindle, Paperback and **Audio**

Dropshipping and Facebook Advertising: Discover How to Make Money Online and Create Passive Income Streams With Dropshipping and Social Media Marketing

This is a **2-in-1 book bundle** consisting of the below books and split into 2 parts. Amazon will make the kindle edition available to you for FREE when you purchase the print version of this bundle from Amazon.com - **saving you roughly 25%** from the price of the individual paperbacks.

- Dropshipping – Discover How to Make Money Online, Build Sustainable Streams of Passive Income and Gain Financial Freedom Using The Dropshipping E-Commerce Business Model (Part 1)
- Facebook Advertising – Learn How to Make $10,000+ Each Month with Facebook Marketing (Part 2)

Available In Kindle, Paperback and **Audio**

Get this bundle at a 35% discount from Amazon.com

Real Estate Investing For Beginners: Earn Passive Income With Reits, Tax Lien Certificates, Lease, Residential & Commercial Real Estate

In this book, Amazon bestselling author, Michael Ezeanaka, provides a step-by-step analysis of 10 Real Estate business models that have the potential to earn you passive income. A quick overview of each business is presented and their liquidity, scalability, potential return on investment, passivity and simplicity are explored.

In this book, you'll discover:

- How to make money with Real Estate Investment Trusts – including an analysis of the impact of the economy on the income from REITs (**Chapter 1**)
- A step-by-step description of how a Real Estate Investment Groups works and how to make money with this business model (**Chapter 2**)
- How to become a limited partner and why stakeholders can influence the running of a Real Estate Limited Partnership even though they have no direct ownership control in it (**Chapter 3**)
- How to protect yourself as a general partner (**Chapter 3**)
- Why tax lien certificates are one of the most secure investments you can make and how to diversify your portfolio of tax lien certificates (**Chapter 4**)
- Strategies you can employ to earn passive income from an empty land (**Chapter 5**)
- Two critical factors that are currently boosting the industrial real estate market and how you can take advantage of them (**Chapter 6**)
- Some of the most ideal locations to set up industrial real estate properties in the US, Asia and Europe (**Chapter 6**)
- Why going for long term leases (instead of short term ones) can significantly increase you return on investment from your industrial real estate properties (**Chapter 6**)
- Why commercial properties can serve as an excellent hedge against inflation – including two ways you can make money with commercial properties (**Chapter 7**)
- How long term leases and potential 'turnover rents' can earn you significant sums of money from Retail real estate properties and why they are very sensitive to the state of the economy (**Chapter 8**)
- More than 10 zoning rights you need to be aware of when considering investing in Mixed-Use properties (**Chapter 9**)
- 100 Tips for success that will help you minimize risks and maximize returns on your real estate investments

And much, much more!

PLUS, **BONUS MATERIALS**: you can download the author's Real Estate Business Scorecard which neatly summarizes, in alphabetical order, each business model's score across those 5 criteria i.e. liquidity, scalability, potential return on investment, passivity and simplicity!

Finally, because this book is enrolled in Kindle Matchbook Program, the **kindle edition of this book will be available to you for free** when you purchase the paperback version from Amazon.com.

If you're ready to take charge of your financial future, grab your copy of This Book today!

Available In <u>Kindle</u>, <u>Paperback</u> and **<u>Audio</u>**

Credit Card And Credit Repair Secrets: Discover How To Repair Your Credit, Get A 700+ Credit Score, Access Business Startup Funding, And Travel For Free Using Reward Cards

Are you sick and tired of paying huge interests on loans due to poor credit scores? Are you frustrated with not knowing where or how to get the necessary capital you need to start your business? Would you like to get all these as well as discover how you can travel the world for FREE?

If so, you'll love Credit Card and Credit Repair Secrets.

Imagine knowing simple do-it-yourself strategies you can employ to repair your credit profile, protect it from identity theft, access very cheap and affordable funding for your business and travel the world without any out of pocket expense!

This can be your reality. You can learn how to do all these and more. Moreover, you may be surprised by how simple doing so is.

In this book, you'll discover:

- **3 Types of consumer credit (And How You Can Access Them!)**
- How To Read, Review and Understand Your Credit Report (Including a Sample Letter You Can Send To Dispute Any Inaccuracy In It)
- **How To Achieve a 700+ Credit Score (And What To Do If You Have No FICO Score)**
- How To Monitor Your Credit Score (Including the difference between hard and soft inquiries)
- **What The VantageScore Model Is, It's Purpose, And How It Differs From The FICO Score Model**
- The Factors That Impact Your Credit Rating. Including The Ones That Certainly Don't - Despite What People Say!
- **Which Is More Important: Payment History Or Credit Utilization? (The Answer May Surprise You)**
- Why You Should Always Check Your Credit Report (At least Once A Month!)
- **How Credit Cards Work (From The Business And Consumer Perspective)**
- Factors You Need To Consider When Choosing A Credit Card (Including How To Avoid A Finance Charge on Your Credit Card)
- **How To Climb The Credit Card Ladder And Unlock Reward Points**
- Which Is More Appropriate: A Personal or Business Credit Card? (Find Out!)
- **How to Protect Your Credit Card From Identity Theft**
- Sources of Fund You Can Leverage To Grow Your Business

And much, much more!

An Identity Theft Resource Center (ITRC) report shows that 1,579 data breaches exposed about 179 million identity records in 2017. Being a victim of an identity scam can cause you a lot of problems. One of the worst cases would be the downfall of your credit score. You don't have to fall victim to it.

This book gives you a simple, but incredibly effective, step-by-step process you can use to build, protect and leverage your stellar credit profile to enjoy a financially stress-free life! It's practical. It's actionable. And if you follow it closely, it'll deliver extraordinary results!

PLUS BONUS - because this book is enrolled in Kindle Matchbook Program, the **kindle edition of this book will be available to you for free** when you purchase the paperback version from Amazon.com.

If you're ready to take charge of your financial future, grab your copy of This Book today!

Available In Kindle, Paperback and **Audio**

Real Estate Investing And Credit Repair: Discover How To Earn Passive Income With Real Estate, Repair Your Credit, Fund Your Business, And Travel For Free Using Reward Credit Cards

This is a **2-in-1 book bundle** consisting of the below books and split into 2 parts. Amazon will make the kindle edition available to you for FREE when you purchase the print version of this bundle from Amazon.com - **saving you roughly 25%** from the price of the individual paperbacks.

- Real Estate Investing For Beginners – Earn Passive Income With Reits, Tax Lien Certificates, Lease, Residential & Commercial Real Estate (Part 1)
- Credit Card And Credit Repair Secrets – Discover How To Repair Your Credit, Get A 700+ Credit Score, Access Business Startup Funding, And Travel For Free Using Reward Cards (Part 2)

Available In Kindle, Paperback and **Audio**

Get this bundle at a 35% discount from Amazon.com

Passive Income With Dividend Investing: Your Step-By-Step Guide To Make Money In The Stock Market Using Dividend Stocks

Have you always wanted to put your money to work in the stock market and earn passive income with dividend stocks?

What would you be able to achieve with a step-by-step guide designed to help you grow your money, navigate the dangers in the stock market and minimize the chance of losing your capital?

Imagine not having to rely solely on a salary or a pension to survive. Imagine having the time, money and freedom to pursue things you're passionate about, whether it's gardening, hiking, reading, restoring a classic car or simply spending time with your loved ones.

This book can help you can create this lifestyle for yourself and your loved ones!

Amazon bestselling author, Michael Ezeanaka, takes you through a proven system that'll help you to build and grow a sustainable stream of passive dividend income. He'll show you, step by step, how to identify stocks to purchase, do accurate due diligence, analyze the impact of the economy on your portfolio and when to consider selling.

In this book, you'll discover:

- Why investing in dividend stocks can position you to benefit tremendously from the "Baby Boomer Boost" (Chapter 1)
- **Which certain industry sectors tend to have a higher dividend payout ratio and why? (Chapter 2)**
- How to time your stock purchase around ex-dividend dates so as to take advantage of discounted share prices (Chapter 2)
- **Why a stock that is showing growth beyond its sustainable rate may indicate some red flags. (Chapter 2)**
- 5 critical questions you need to ask in order to assess if a company's debt volume will affect your dividend payment (Chapter 3)
- **How high dividend yield strategy can result in low capital gain taxes (Chapter 4)**
- Reasons why the average lifespan of a company included in the S&P 500 plummeted from 67 years in the 1920s to just 15 years in 2015. (Chapter 5)
- **A blueprint for selecting good dividend paying stocks (Chapter 6)**
- The vital information you need to look out for when reading company financial statements (Chapter 7)
- **A strategy you can use to remove the emotion from investing, as well as, build wealth cost efficiently (Chapter 8)**
- An affordable way to diversify your portfolio if you have limited funds (Chapter 9)
- **Why you may want to think carefully before selling cyclical stocks with high P/E ratio (Chapter 10)**

And much, much more!

PLUS BONUS - because this book is enrolled in Kindle Matchbook Program, the **kindle edition of this book will be available to you for free** when you purchase the paperback version from Amazon.com.

Whether you're a student, corporate executive, entrepreneur, or stay-at-home parent, the tactics described in this book can set the stage for a financial transformation.

If you're ready to build and grow a steady stream of passive dividend income, Grab your copy of this book today!

Available In <u>Kindle,</u> <u>Paperback</u> and **<u>Audio</u>**

Appendix A

Solution to Chapter 1 Quiz

Question Number	Answer
1	B
2	C
3	A
4	A
5	B
6	B
7	B
8	D
9	A
10	A

Appendix B

Solution to Chapter 2 Quiz

Question Number	Answer
1	A
2	C
3	D
4	A
5	A
6	A
7	D
8	A

9	A
10	A

Appendix C

Solution to Chapter 3 Quiz

Question Number	Answer
1	A
2	D
3	A
4	D
5	A
6	A
7	B
8	A
9	B
10	D

Appendix D

Solution to Chapter 4 Quiz

Question Number	Answer
1	A
2	B
3	A
4	B

5	B
6	A
7	B
8	C
9	A
10	D

Appendix E

Solution to Chapter 5 Quiz

Question Number	Answer
1	A
2	B
3	A
4	C
5	B
6	C
7	C
8	A
9	A
10	C

Appendix F

Solution to Chapter 6 Quiz

Question Number	Answer
1	C
2	A
3	A
4	B
5	D
6	C
7	B
8	C
9	B
10	D

Appendix G

Solution to Chapter 7 Quiz

Question Number	Answer
1	D
2	C
3	A
4	A
5	D
6	A

7	D
8	C
9	A
10	D

Appendix H

Solution to Chapter 8 Quiz

Question Number	Answer
1	D
2	B
3	D
4	C
5	C
6	D
7	C
8	A
9	C
10	C

Appendix I

Solution to Chapter 9 Quiz

Question Number	Answer
1	C
2	A

3	B
4	C
5	B
6	B
7	B
8	D
9	C
10	A

Appendix J

Solution to Chapter 10 Quiz

Question Number	Answer
1	B
2	C
3	B
4	A
5	B
6	B
7	C
8	B
9	A
10	A

Appendix K

Solution to Chapter 11 Quiz

Question Number	Answer
1	C
2	C
3	A
4	B
5	A
6	A
7	A
8	A
9	D
10	A

Appendix L

Solution to Chapter 12 Quiz

Question Number	Answer
1	C
2	B
3	D
4	A
5	C
6	A
7	D

8	C
9	D
10	A

Appendix M

Solution to Chapter 13 Quiz

Question Number	Answer
1	A
2	C
3	A
4	C
5	A
6	A
7	A
8	D
9	A
10	D

www.ingramcontent.com/pod-product-compliance
Lightning Source LLC
Chambersburg PA
CBHW061326190326
41458CB00011B/3916